Your Calling
as a
Christian

SEE ALSO

Your Calling as an Elder
Gary Straub

———————

Your Calling as a Deacon
Gary Straub and James Trader II

———————

Your Calling as a Leader
Gary Straub and Judy G. Turner

Available at
www.chalicepress.com

Your Calling
as a
Christian

Timothy L. Carson

CHALICE
PRESS
ST. LOUIS, MISSOURI

Biblical quotations, unless otherwise noted, are from the *New Revised Standard Version Bible*, copyright 1989, Division of Christian Education of the National Council of the Churches of Christ in the United States of America. Used by permission. All rights reserved.

Cover and interior design: Elizabeth Wright

Visit Chalice Press on the World Wide Web at
www.chalicepress.com

10 9 8 7 6 5 4 3 2 1   07 08 09 10 11 12

Library of Congress Cataloging–in–Publication Data

Carson, Timothy L.
  Your calling as a Christian / Tim Carson.
     p. cm.
  ISBN-13: 978-0-8272-4413-9
  1. Christianity. 2. Christian life. I. Title.

  BR123.C37 2007
  248.4–dc22

                                                2006033392

Printed in the United States of America

For the three congregations I have been honored to serve:

Community Christian Church
Camdenton, Missouri

Webster Groves Christian Church
St. Louis, Missouri

University Christian Church
Ft. Worth, Texas

Contents

Introduction

I have no idea how you got your hands on this book, but I'm glad you did. Perhaps a well-meaning friend thought you might find it helpful. Or maybe a pastor sent it your direction because he or she knew you were asking the kind of questions you will find discussed here. It could be that your present congregation is studying this book together, and you just needed to buy one for the course. I don't know how you came by it, but I suppose that doesn't really matter.

What does matter is that we now have an opportunity to share a conversation about some of the most profound questions of life.

You could be exploring these questions of faith for the first time; for you, then, this book is a maiden voyage into the unknown. Or maybe you just have a half-remembered experience of church in your childhood, one that never blossomed, and now, as an adult, you are ready for more.

Possibly, you are one of the millions who discarded religious life and all of its practices early on. But now, later in life, you are giving it another shot because the gap in your gut is telling you to reopen the case.

I know, too, that you could be one of those practicing Christians who just never stops growing. Every so often you like to return to something elemental, basic, and foundational. And you especially enjoy hearing a new take on the old, old story.

Wherever you are, whoever you are, welcome to this exploration or reexploration of what the Christian faith might be and become for you. In past times people might have called this book an *apology*, but not because I'm sorry or asking you to pardon me. The apology has historically served as an argument for or a defense of treasured beliefs in culturally relevant terms. I'll let you be the judge of whether I accomplished that goal here or not.

You might be wondering what to expect from this little excursion. That's a fair question, and I have to answer you on several different levels. First of all, you may find your own questions here. It's a good thing to find your own questions being asked by others, even if they are framed a little differently. Second, you will discover the outlines of the basic themes of the Christian faith. If these are unfamiliar to you, they will serve as an introduction. If they're old hat, they will be a kind of review. Third, you will find yourself poised between contemporary culture and faith. I will encourage those two sides of the aisle to talk to one another. I will also call some prevailing cultural assumptions into question. Fourth, you will find I challenge some of the conventional thinking about Christian theology, because I either don't believe it myself or I believe the old formulations are actually getting in the way of a fresh encounter with God.

It is one thing to consider *what* you might find here. It is quite another thing to consider *who* is doing the writing, so let me tell you. I've been a pastor for a very long time, and I happen to be of the male version of the species. I am married to a very gifted woman, who keeps my feet on the ground. I have a creative and funny daughter, who has lived with deep disabilities all her life. My dog is getting really old, but the cat is still a youngster. I like music, scuba diving, reading, and seeing a good movie. My life revolves around my ministry, and I wouldn't have it any other way.

So you see, the voice you hear in these pages is not one of some omniscient narrator. I'm a real person talking with you. To give you a visual: Most of these words were written in the morning, between six and eight, as I was sitting at my kitchen table, wearing a robe, and drinking a cup of coffee. Imagine me sitting in front of the laptop, gazing into the living room, and wondering who you, the reader, would be. Keep that image in mind.

As you have your own hopes for your life, you have your own hopes for reading this book. My hope is that you will find yet another opportunity to seriously engage with the life-giving power of the Christian faith. If your time browsing through these pages takes you only one more step down the road, I will consider our conversation a great success.

I would be delighted if you found this book to be a page-turner and were unable to resist reading chapter after chapter in one sitting. But you might find a better way. You might instead read one chapter a day just to let it sink in, to give it time to percolate. You will find some scriptural references at the end of each chapter if you want to dig deeper.

Of course, discussion groups can spread these chapters over the course of several weeks as an intentional study. I have led similar weekly study and discussion groups that have revolved around a shared meal.

The most important thing is that the Spirit is always at work and always has been. I know I will be entering your spiritual journey midstream, finding you at different points along the way and more or less receptive to what I have to share with you. That doesn't bother me a bit. I trust that God will be working with you in just the right way for now.

Thanks for joining me on the journey. The honor is mine.

Why Should I Care?

I'm not really a religious person.

But you believe?

> *Not really, not the way you think.*

> But you believe in certain things.

>> *Well, maybe. I think certain things are essential.*

>> Such as?

>>> *Such as the sun is going to come up in the morning.*

>>> *Such as I've got some reason for being here.*

>>> *Such as it's all got to mean something; we just have no idea what.*

>>> Then you have a kind of faith in something?

>>>> *But not like you mean. I could still believe in those things even if all this is a big cosmic accident.*

>> How about science?

It doesn't have all the answers we thought it would, but there is something hopeful about it.

> But you're not going to trust your life to it?

No, it's a human thing that's fallible.

Besides, it discovers little things like atomic power that can be good, but can be used for evil purposes.

By humans.

Who else?

So what about this humanity thing?

What about it?

Do you have faith in humanity?

Are you kidding?

What about all that vast potential we always hear about?

Why would I trust in a species that just can't get enough genocides?

That's not a favorable rating.

No, it's not, and I happen to be one of them.

But humans are more than terror and torture.

Yes, but there is as much to mistrust as to admire.

So why are you so enamored with fantasy video, TV, and cinema?

They're probably an escape.

So *Harry Potter* and *Lord of the Rings* are just escapist?

Well, they say something.

About?

About what could be, another dimension.

Something more.

But not magic—I don't believe in that—or supernatural stuff.

But you like stories of possession like *Stigmata*—that's supernatural—and ghost stories. Why do you get off on that?

I know what that really is—just imagination popping my primal fear.

Why do you get all teary-eyed when you go to a U2 concert?

It's really hopeful.

Hopeful in what?

In something more than all this.

Hope coming from where?

Just dreams, just longings.

So there's something about singing the same song with thousands?

Maybe you get a glimpse of the bigger picture.

But you're a tourist there, aren't you?

You don't normally live with the thousands.

I've got my small circle of friends. That's all I need.

Or all you have.

Whatever.

I can imagine you don't have extensive trust in either government or big business.

They're systems. You live with them. Try to make them better. Endure them. Outwit them. They try to get rich. They try to control or profit from everything they touch.

Cheerful thought.

Isn't it?

And the Web?

A parallel universe.

Is it real?

Kind of. Not exactly real. Not exactly not.

But you live in it.

It lives in the world.

But it's made by humans too.

Yes, so it's just as fallible.

But you find a sense of connection there?

Partially. It offers what it offers.

So why do you keep on watching the Olympics if you don't really like sports?

The international thing.

Aren't those just more governmental systems?

It's the people of those governments who come together.

But just for a moment.

A moment is all we ever have.

Ever want more than that?

Wanting doesn't change reality.

I know the difference between fantasy and reality.

Speaking of fantasy, is that where God belongs?

It's just a word.

So is your name.

I could change my name, and I'd still be me.

God is like that.

Keep talking.

It's a word that points to something beyond it.

So what about the idea of God?

Honestly?

Be brutal.

The deity of popular culture, the institutional church, TV evangelists, and football team prayers—I just can't buy those.

Tell me more about the God you don't believe in.

I don't believe in a Big Old Man in the sky, some Zeus on Mount Olympus throwing lightning bolts.

I don't believe in a Divine Master Puppeteer pulling all the strings on all the little drones in the anthill.

I don't accept a God who has suffering as a part of the plan.

I don't believe in the tribal God, sending hocus-pocus to make us win while the other guy bites the dust.

I don't believe in that god either.

But you call yourself a Christian?

I discarded those concepts of god long ago. But I also don't believe in some flat, two-dimensional, mechanical, disenchanted universe either.

If you don't buy that all that stuff, but still have faith, what's the alternative?

That's what I want to talk to you about.

For Further Reflection

Ecclesiastes 1:1–9   What does it all mean?

I Know, I Know

How do we know what we know? When it comes to the spiritual dimensions of life, this question gets tricky. We assume so many things, or don't. What can we trust? Is it a matter of garnering the right information? What does it mean to "know" something, anyway? People make lots of claims about knowing God, but can they be trusted? Why? How do you come to conclusions about anything? Through the senses? Deep intuitions? Reasoned arguments? Interpretations of the world provided by the culture? The ideas held by language itself?

One of the ways religious people have attempted to simplify believing in a complex world is to just cut themselves off from other fields of thought. By shelving science, for example, they could eliminate any challenges to their worldview and any alternative way of knowing. This separation has been a common strategy ever since the rise of the Enlightenment in the seventeenth century: dividing religion and science into parallel universes. The two cousins certainly have different aims, methods, and dramatically different language, but do we really live in such a segmented universe? Does belief in one automatically require disregard for the other?

If people of faith divide existence into the measurable content of science, which would be anything in the natural world, and the immeasurable aspects of life into the realm of the spiritual or supernatural, what is the result? Every time science discovers one more explanation about the natural world, the spiritual domain shrinks in direct proportion. In other words, whenever a religious explanation is superseded by a natural explanation that doesn't need God in the formula, the religious conviction becomes obsolete. This way of dividing up the things we know becomes a huge problem.

This two-state solution to the ways religion and science know what they know implies that people of faith shouldn't have anything to say about brain research, for example, and its correlation to things of the Spirit. Physicists can make remarkable discoveries about the intricate and wondrous structures, forces, and interrelationships of the world; but a world partitioned into science and religion will not allow for a serious religious dialogue with those very same discoveries.

Although religion and science are different and have different purposes, a kind of apartheid of knowledge is doomed to fail us. In the end, a religious separatism, an absolute distancing of religious ways of knowing from other ways of knowing (philosophy, sociology, psychology, art) exiles religion into a disconnected and often irrelevant corner. There has to be another way.

Even as religious persons hold on to their treasured traditions and way of knowing, they must move beyond a posture of either ignoring or attacking other ways of knowing the universe. These are not helpful. With courage they must be willing and able to interpret the other ways, engage with them, sometimes challenge their presuppositions, and in some cases revise their own understanding of God as a result. It took a Galileo to bring about a revolution of knowledge in the medieval church; the sun didn't revolve around the earth after all.

For example, evolutionary biologists do not need God as part of the explanation of their system. In fact, according to their method, God is outside of their province altogether. But Christians may look at this amazing evolutionary process and see something not seen to others: a manifestation of the divine creativity. People of faith may look at these millions of years of the world's creation with holy wonder. They believe God moves in decisive moments in history but is also at the center of huge and vast unfolding processes. Both of these manifestations deserve a hymn of praise. And so the world of faith intentionally remains in a conversation with the many ways of knowing.

How does one come to know things about God in the first place? One way to begin our exploration of that question is to invite some engaging conversation partners to join us.

Our first guest is Thomas Aquinas, arguably the most influential theologian of the medieval church. His thoughts have shaped much of Christian thought for centuries.

TC (TIM CARSON): Welcome and thank you for so powerfully contributing to this whole conversation about how one knows God in the first place. Dr. Aquinas, please tell us a little about how God is known in human existence. Is the divine life something that can be known by anyone without, say, the aid of religious categories? Are we talking about reason here or some kind of deduction from observation?

TA (THOMAS AQUINAS): Yes, I think that even a nonreligious person, one who does not have the particular knowledge received by Christian faith through the scriptures, may deduce many things on the basis of reason alone. Any intelligent person who rationally considers the world and its structures may perceive a First Cause or Original Mover standing behind it all.

TC: So one may know the Builder by the resulting projects?

TA: Precisely. One simply deduces that something comes from somewhere, emerges from a source, just like everything else does.

TC: But are there things that cannot be known on this basis?

TA: Indeed. Take your current evolutionary biologists or string theorists, for instance. They can surmise nothing about how this originated, or more importantly, why. From reason alone you cannot move backwards to the divine love or purposes of God. That must be discovered and known differently.

TC: So reason might take one so far, but no farther?

TA: What you do know through reason may be partial and fragmentary at best. Your deductions about the First Mover are inevitably incomplete. I might look at the house across the street and think of basic things about the builder: He had the skill and knowledge to build such a structure; the requisite skill to do so was present; he had some motivation for doing it in the first place. I am somehow even capable and motivated to ask these questions in the first place. But other than these I have little more to say. Except for some level of appreciation, this bare minimum of knowledge in no way demands any kind of change in my life, nor does it require any special kind of response from me.

TC: So what can complete the picture?

TA: The only way the picture can be completed, the fragments assembled, and distortions corrected is through the self-revelation of God to us. By that I mean God has to reveal God's nature for us to understand. This understanding requires more than observation of the natural order and forming conclusions from that. God's nature can only be known as God reveals it to us. If we really are to know the actual builder who made the house across the street, the builder will have to come, knock on our door, and tell us all about himself or herself.

TC: Thank you, Dr. Aquinas. Now I would like to invite John Calvin into our conversation. As you know, Dr. Calvin is the great Protestant reformer of sixteenth-century Geneva. Welcome and thank you for sharing your convictions and insights. How does your thinking about this compare to that of your predecessor Dr. Aquinas?

JC (JOHN CALVIN): I take the critique of reason quite a bit further. The problem is not only that our reason is fragmentary or that aspects of truth remain inaccessible by reason alone. The problem lies in the ways our reason has been damaged and twisted by human nature itself.

TC: You mean that the mechanism of reason itself is flawed and untrustworthy?

JC: Yes. It's not merely that the lens of the telescope is not strong enough to see into the distance. The problem is that there is a stigmatism in the lens that distorts the incoming information. The result is that the incoming signal cannot be trusted.

TC: This stigmatism in the lens has to do with human nature itself?

JC: Correct. Our own inclination to self-centeredness twists any information so that reason always leaves our understanding disoriented. People think they are seeing correctly, but the knower is oblivious to the ways sight is distorted.

TC: Well, it sounds like our psychic processor is out of whack, some kind of impaired perception.

JC: That's how you might put it. But think of it this way: Human beings can indeed have a natural sense of God; they may perceive a craftsman behind the world or even intuitively sense the presence of God. On this, Aquinas is right. Just think of all the world religions that have sprung up everywhere in all times; these religions are evidence of such intuitions and longings. The way in which nonreligious people instinctively turn beyond themselves in times of crisis convinces us even more. But that said, the distortion of reason due to our flawed lens means none of these intuitions or longings are in themselves sufficient or lead to anything enduring. I may perceive something, sense something, but not know what it means. Like my viewing of the sparks shooting up from a campfire, I first may be amazed with their flaring, but they always and inevitably disappear into the night.

TC: Then nature by itself does not give a clue?

JC: Only if you live by faith already. For the one who knows God, nature becomes the theater of God's glory. But without the knowledge of God the observation of nature alone cannot lead to faith unaided. The lens of human perception is too distorted and the God we know too hidden. The creature can never fully know the creator who has created it without help.

TC: What kind of help?

JC: If I am an old man and my eyesight is failing, you may hand me a book, and I will know it is a book. But if I open it, my eyes simply cannot read the text inside. I need a pair of spectacles so that I can see what is written. The spectacles are for us the revelation of God through Christ. Now we can see.

TC: Thank you Dr. Calvin. It is a pleasure to welcome our next guest, none other than John Wesley, the progenitor of the modern Methodist movement. One of the things for which you are known, Mr. Wesley, is your description of the ways in which a person may come to know God. You present what has been called a "quadrilateral," a fourfold model of sources of authority that might lead one to God. Could you tell us about that, and how it might be similar to or different from the perspectives of Dr. Aquinas and Dr. Calvin?

JC: (JOHN WESLEY): Like Aquinas I understand reason as a pathway to God, but only reason sanctified by a faithful heart, one seeking God for God's sake. Like Calvin I understand reason must be accompanied by other forces of faith to make it whole. Where I differ is in the ways that multiple sources of knowing actually work together.

TC: What is the fourfold model?

JW: Scripture, tradition, reason, and experience.

TC: And how do they work together?

JW: You can enter through any one among the four, but you also need to seriously engage with the other three. For instance, I may have one of Calvin's sparks in the night experience, but the witness of scripture helps me understand the holiness of God in the world, and reflection on tradition allows me to listen to all those who have thought deeply about this before. My reason makes sense of the structure and purposes of the divine world.

TC: Is there a priority among the four?

JW: One could say they all fall without scripture, which is the primary testimony of the people of God. You could live with less of the other three, but without scripture you're in trouble. I trust experience more than my preceding conversation partners. God is working in the heart through a person's experience, which often leads to the search for a more reasoned, grounded, and full revelation of God.

TC: If I am searching for God and my heart becomes strangely warmed, as did yours, what will lead me to know God more fully?

JW: The Holy Spirit will guide you into a more complete understanding, one that is united with the truth and power of the scriptures and the testimony of God's people.

TC: It so happens that Alexander Campbell, often thought to be the first among equals of the founders of the Disciples of Christ, has entered the room. Welcome, Elder Campbell. So where does one begin in knowing God?

AC (ALEXANDER CAMPBELL): The first thing you have to know about me is that I believe the rational structures of the mind are a gift of God and meant to lead toward the maker who created them. By rational thought and discourse one may reasonably approach the nature of God, interpret the scriptures, and understand the message of our faith. So today I find myself in an unusual place.

TC: Unusual?

AC: Yes, I am aligned in strange ways with your other guests. I find myself closer to Aquinas than I would like to admit! Reason does take us to the places we need to go, though it cannot provide all the content we need. Its primary function is certainly not to reinforce doctrines. But I have to say I am much less persuaded by Calvin, my elder cousin by whom I have been shaped and from whom I have moved great distances. Reason is much more trustworthy than he believes, though I admit it requires a faithful intent to apply it.

TC: You are known for your distrust of experience.

AC: Yes, and for that reason I have my greatest difficulty with Mr. Wesley and those like him. A person can have lots of experiences—holy and unholy—but they may not say a thing about God. I mistrust experience to the same degree that Calvin mistrusts reason. So many on the American frontier had all manner of ecstatic experiences in our revival movements. I always considered them with great caution. One does not need a cataclysmic emotional experience to be convicted about the truth of gospel through the scriptures. Truth appears by the force of reason and will. As a matter of fact, I believe the duo of scripture and reason always trumps and critiques tradition and experience.

In the centuries following the lives of these Christian thinkers, people have alternately embraced or rejected all these claims to knowing God. The landscape is baffling indeed, and this is hyper-true in our own day.

Secular voices take apart the large religious narratives, their claims, authority structures, and hierarchy and urge the culture to create a world without God. Sociologists attribute all religious forms to cultural creation and shaping. Psychologists identify the psychological mechanisms that cause people to either create gods for their own security or surrender their autonomy to group movements. Evolutionary biologists explain a physical unfolding of nature that does not require divine mechanisms. Liberationists suspect all authority because of its propensity to take power for its own interests.

But do not be misled: This instantaneously communicative, high-tech, multicultural, globalized, complex world has become anything but secular. The words of the Dali Lama or Confucius or Ramakrishna are becoming just as familiar to many Americans as those of Moses or Jesus of Nazareth. People are living and dying because of their religion. As I write this sentence, many Muslims throughout the world are rioting because Muhammad was lampooned in a recent newspaper cartoon. At the same time powerful Christian coalitions continue their attempt to control the political center of culture. Fundamentalist movements continue to arise, moving against modernity and relativism, making absolutist claims about faith and drawing large constituencies.

People flock to hear the latest preacher du jour in huge stadium gatherings. People are, as in no time before, swimming in a vast sea of religious claims and movements.

On a quieter level, a search for deep connection with the universe continues unabated. Young people explore the many world religions. Mystics lead their adherents into deep worlds of meditation and prayer. Baby boomers who cast off the church as irrelevant a generation earlier are returning to take another look. Creative minds and hearts are taking time-honored religious truths and redressing them in the music and images of alternative culture.

How, then, could a person ever decide about such weighty issues? How could one know which path is a legitimate one? The temptation is to simply turn them into objects of interesting inquiry and walk away. But what if you are genuinely seeking, wanting to plug into the circuit board of the universe?

Can a person really "know" God in the way we use that word? What does it mean to have a relationship with God when you know it will barely resemble the connections you have with your spouse or child or friend?

Whatever language or metaphor or poetry we use to describe this awareness of and connection to the power behind and within the universe, it is invariably lacking. It is simply impossible to adequately name this windstorm we name God. Whether we appeal to the ancient wisdom or to contemporary experience, knowing where to begin may seem impossible. How do you know?

For Further Reflection

Job 38:1–4	The limits of our understanding
John 18:37–38	What is truth?
John 10:14–15	Knowing all around
Romans 8:15–16	The Spirit speaking through us

The Unique Christian Path

Isn't the Christian Path Just Another Moral Code?

I can imagine you wondering, "Why Christianity? I try to be a good person, a good citizen, and an ethical person. I volunteer with civic organizations following hurricanes. Why should I want or need anything more? I'm a pretty well-read person. I know what the great religions have said about love or justice or care for the earth. According to my own standards, I know the difference between right and wrong. I recycle. I drive a hybrid rather than an SUV. And all things considered, I'm really not so sure Christianity has a monopoly on morals as compared with other religions. Even if I did believe that the Christian faith had some superior moral ethic, you will never convince me that through the centuries it's even come close to fulfilling its ideals. I see a pretty significant performance gap. So why should I pay it any mind?"

All the living religions of the world have a strong ethical component; how you treat your neighbor or live in harmony with the earth matters. Your moral decisions serve as a strong indication of your character and values. Not only that, but the living religions lift up high moral standards and insist they are good not only for the one but also for the many. This assertion can hardly be disputed.

Does the Christian faith offer something distinct, something that might stand apart from the pack? To be honest, the Christian way *is* similar to other religious paths in many respects. For instance, it joins other faiths in professing an ethic of the golden rule, that one should treat the neighbor as one would want to be treated. Like many other world religions the Christian faith elevates such virtues as mercy, justice, compassion, self-sacrifice, and love. Indeed, in these ways practicing Christians may resemble observant persons of other faiths.

Some might try to make an argument for God by pointing to universal moral principles that underlie human existence. They would point to principles found in such notable documents as the preamble to the American *Declaration of Independence,* which states that certain truths are self-evident; they are woven into the way things are. Those well-meaning founders and others like them were Deists; they believed that a working set of universal principles is writ large in the cosmos. If you just search long enough, you'll find them.

If you *do* subscribe to this understanding of universal principles, you could easily assume that these principles are why most religious paths naturally teach and embody similar moral absolutes. This understanding has been one of the frequent arguments for the commonality of all religions, and many people have appealed to it.

But how do you explain the differences? However much the great religions share many of the same ethical principles, they also hold distinct convictions, tenets peculiar to their unique view of reality. In this sense the great religious traditions are not merely tapping into the same pipeline of universal principles. Just as often they hold diverse points of view. One religion may view war one way while its cousin views it otherwise. One faith holds that God somehow acts in history toward one end while another doesn't believe a deity exists to do the acting. As similar as religions are, they are also remarkably different.

The difference in how Christians approach this sense of the moral imperative, of a deep, ethical life, has to do with the *why*. The *why* is directly related to the larger Christian story, and a good case can be made that you really can't understand the Christian ethic apart from this larger story. That is, the Christian faith is not, at its core, a list of moral maxims that simply reflect the master list you can find inscribed anywhere in the cosmos. As opposed to what Thomas Jefferson would have liked, Christianity is not like a pot of soup in which you can boil away the embarrassing aspects of the story to reveal the true consumé of morals in the bottom of the pot.

No, the soup is the thing; the whole Christian story presents a way of God acting in the world that elicits a certain kind of response by those who are grabbed by it. Moral response follows the dawning awareness of what God is up to in the world and among those who have fallen in love with God. It is not pursued first and by itself, as a way to accomplish something apart from the lead story of God's action. In the Christian faith, the moral life emerges as an imperative of response: I must because God has. Then I am set free.

The Christian faith is not primarily about being a nice person, though nice is better than not nice. Many nonreligious people are nice, ethical, generous, and caring. The Christian way does not first define itself by what it means to be good, though being good is much better than being otherwise. The Christian faith first tells a story of God working in wondrous ways in the world; everything that follows is our attempt to join in that story.

When you choose to first evaluate the validity of the Christian faith with a comparison of moral or ethical systems, you have chosen the wrong starting place. If you insist on starting there, you will inevitably misjudge and misunderstand the Christian faith, and by extension, compare it with other faiths incorrectly.

Christians share a particular understanding of holy love, the highest of spiritual states and practices. Christians understand that godly love transcends everything else. We know it because we have been the recipients of God's love. The question then becomes, How might one become a person of such love? Is it by making a list of loving qualities and straining to imitate them? Is it to deny everything that is not love? Is this achieved by huffing and puffing and willing love into being?

Here is the secret, from a Christian point of view: This highest of ideals is impossible, at least by human efforts. Godly love only becomes possible by a grace that reveals the beautiful and mysterious vision of life transcending anything we can see or know. For Christians this mystery is bound up in the love of God revealed in Christ. Only this love, we believe, allows us to remotely fulfill the radical claim of love on our lives. Without Christ's love we just end up following a set of rules. With it we are given the desire to begin loving God in return, and in that we find our joy and peace and reason for following.

I Find God in Nature, and for Me That's Enough.

"I just love nature." That's how many describe their experience of God. What this kind of statement indicates in the popular mind is that nature is a stand in for God. That notion is called *pantheism.*

What is wrong with understanding God through nature?

There is nothing wrong with apprehending the sacred through the various manifestations of the natural order. The problem enters when nature *becomes* God. Why isn't that enough for Christians?

Most first peoples, indigenous cultures, have close and sacred relationships with the natural world. Most often their natural world is imbued with spiritual forces and powers. In most primitive forms these powers act on and are placated by the rituals, prayers, and ceremonies of the believers. In one way or another the people have designed religious responses around either heading off malevolent spirits or beckoning benevolent ones.

On the other hand, most technological, Enlightenment-shaped, mechanistic worldview persons are profoundly estranged from the natural world. They may experience it vicariously through media, or consider it when a natural disaster raises its ugly head, or even partake of its pleasures through sport or recreation. But that doesn't change the way they view nature or their relationship to it. Like most in the modern world, the industrio-techno person is profoundly estranged from nature. As a result of that loss of connection, nature becomes an object, something of which they are not a part, another commodity to be used, exploited, and controlled. But they have little conscious relationship with nature or their place within the web of nature. That gap is a profound one. So before saying anything else, we should first remember just how alienated we have become from the planet that sustains us and to which our bodies shall return. People of faith have a special responsibility for care of the gift of creation in which we live.

That disclaimer made, we can return to the question of why Christians are not pantheists. Pantheism claims that God *is* nature, or vice versa. Pantheism is wanting for many reasons, not the least of which is that it doesn't allow freedom for the purposeful power of God to be or to act before, beyond, or outside of natural forces. To equate God with natural forces is to limit God to them or to make God into another, albeit larger and grander, thing. Instead Christians claim the creating force of the universe is beyond that which is created.

In the beginning, in the place of origins, God was and God created. God is still creating and unfolding in the process of creation. Indeed, a person can know much of God through the natural order. But Christians also believe God transcends nature. Behind the mask of nature is a greater power. Imploding stars can obliterate an entire solar system, but God still is.

We can easily conclude too much from the beauty of nature. When we find the sunrise beautiful, and the mountains and trees and brooks delightful, we may be inspired and rightfully so. But it is easy to push that appreciation to a place Christians find untenable.

For example, Romantics such as John Keats took this appreciation of nature a step further as they understood beauty to be equivalent to truth and vice versa. If that is the case, a subjective experience of what is pleasing becomes the highest religious experience, the definition of truth and even of God. Ralph Waldo Emerson and the other New England Transcendentalists found God's true sanctuary not in houses or religious systems built by human hands, but rather in the raw stuff of hill and tree and brook and species. Henry David Thoreau lived on Walden Pond for two years and found the Spirit in the coming and going of the predictable seasons and nature's weaving of the natural tapestry.

To that Christians might say, "Yes, but ..." Yes, we understand that God is beyond our human-made systems and social arrangements, but we also understand that God is beyond nature itself.

Imagine that, following a thrilling view of an ocean sunset, you promptly slip into a deep crevice from the most recent earthquake, or watch your city slide under the dark waters of the hurricane, or flee for your life as your house tumbles off a cliff in a mudslide. Now what do you make of a nature-God? The way you answer this question will clarify how you understand God.

To rationalize this dissonance you might claim God is punishing humans with natural forces. The only problem with that point of view is that a forest fire doesn't discriminate; it is not selective, burning the good and the bad in its path. A hurricane blows away the saints and sinners both.

In an act of intellectual gymnastics you might assign everything good to God and everything hurtful to the devil. In that case though, you end up with two nature gods like the animists, one good and one evil, or two sides of the same god like the dualists, a kind of yin and yang, Dr. Jekyll and Mr. Hyde god.

You see the problem that is arising. Life itself undermines the definition of God as nature and nature as God.

Perhaps the natural disaster awakens you to the obvious fact that nature is absolutely indifferent to the human plight. As a result of this, you may begin to realize that you view various disasters from a subjective human point of view and from that assign to nature qualities of the good, the bad, or the ugly. Seen objectively, the world is much more than beautiful spacious skies and amber waves of grain. On the contrary, the whole world is always consuming itself. You can soften it by calling it the food chain, but the reality is that somebody is always eating somebody else for lunch.

Nature can indeed be beautiful, spacious, and awe-inspiring. It can also be terrifying, hostile, and brutal. And that's just one reason that Christians resist equating God with nature and reducing God to nature. That definition is much too small and confuses the source with the multiple ways in which it is manifested. In the end, Christians understand that the glory of God shines through creation but is never limited to it. That is some of what we Christians mean when we say God is *transcendent*: participating in the world while not limited to it.

Put differently, energy never goes away; it just changes form and function. It would be a big mistake to confuse the form and structure of matter with its underlying energy. In the same way we Christians don't confuse the form of nature with the energy that underlies it.

God moves beyond every category of what we experience and know in the sensory world. Believing in nature is not enough. We have to know God and God's purposes in the cosmos through other means. Then we might begin to speak of *nature's God*.

I Just Pick and Choose the Spiritual Pieces I Need. I Don't Need a Tradition.

I once knew a person who described herself as *spiritually promiscuous*. By that she meant she had a series of love affairs with various spiritual traditions to see what she could find. She didn't love any one tradition exclusively and never remained there for an extended time. Rather, she scavenged body parts that suited her from each of her lovers and assembled these random philosophical and religious bites into her ideal eclectic thing. That, said she, was her "spirituality."

Of course, there is much to be commended for dialogue with other faiths, exploring the multiple claims to truth, and listening to the autobiographical spiritual narratives of others. There is much to learn. God speaks in many ways. The understandings of our own tradition may be clarified, enriched, or modified. Many forms lead to the formlessness beyond them all.

But the problem with the eclectic construction approach arrives from the method itself. As one fishes for fragments of truth here, there, and everywhere, the pieces are not necessarily complimentary to one another, and are often distorted and trivialized when removed from the original context of their own religious traditions.

For instance, the God of the Native American spirit quest or sweat lodge ritual is not the same un-god of Buddhism. One might argue for common ultimate ends, but if one were to pick up a practice or two from either tradition without carefully examining each one's core philosophies or beliefs, the traditions will inevitably begin to contradict one another—not on an experiential level at first but eventually on an intellectual one. They hold not only different practices but also very different claims about the existence of God and the way God might act or be in the world. These practices often derive from the larger understandings of God and the universe. Even if the practices are relatively complementary, sitting in Zen practice of meditation or engaging in the dream journey of the sweat lodge, one still has to ask the ultimate questions: In which am I participating? What kind of God is at work here? And how do I relate to that? If your answer is that they both work, then you will need to ask exactly how the two notions of God work together. This is the first challenge of the bits and pieces approach to an eclectic spirituality. The second has to do with integrity.

Every religious tradition has, as a part of its overall understanding of the sacred, the way the universe works, the way humans find their way to God, and a series of practices. These devotional, ritual, and communal practices lead the way to deeper faith and a stronger resolve to fulfill and live the truth of the tradition. But these practices find their meaning in connection with the sacred understandings of the larger tradition. They were given birth by the tradition and are passed on by the tradition.

Consider the Quaker path of quietism. Out of silence the Friends share an extemporaneous word from the Spirit in the midst of the gathered community. A particular understanding of revelation is at work here. If you subscribe to this spiritual discipline and the way the Spirit speaks to the community, you will grant a sense of authority to such utterances. What this practice is *not* is just a quiet time for people to share opinions; that is something altogether different. To tear this Quaker practice from its theological moorings would not only be to distort it, but also to disrespect it. The particular practice is held and shaped by the understandings of the tradition.

A person may construct a list of all the spiritual bits and pieces that are enjoyable, desirable, and perhaps exotic— a native American prayer here, a Muslim hajj there, a Sufi dance today, an Orthodox procession with incense tomorrow. If the person then uses and practices these spiritual acts disconnected from their traditions of origin, they will inevitably be distorted and emptied of their true power: How do they meaningfully fit together? How does one understand the meaning of each?

It's not wrong to learn, appreciate, wonder, and even participate in any or all of these. Beyond all of these forms may be the formless reality to which they point. But if one is to realize an integrated and comprehensive way of faith, it will not be by uprooting religious plants from their own native soil and transplanting them in a window box. Not only that, this practice of borrowing religious bits and pieces does not honor the traditions from whence they have come. It usually trivializes them. That's the worse case scenario of a sloppy universalism.

I Have a Personal Spirituality; I'm Not a Religious Person.

Some people seek a "pure" spirituality, unfettered by religious traditions or their frameworks. They are seeking the essence of spirituality, the straight stuff. You may have heard, or said yourself, something like this: "There is a difference between spirituality and religion. When you get into religion you are into a human construction; spirituality is personal and private, my direct connection to God." Most often the speaker means that subjective experience is the real thing, the substance of spirituality.

The personal intuitions, longings, and questing of the heart are important signs of the creature longing for creator, the wandering heart heading for home. Mystics from all times have lost themselves in the vastness and mystery of God. They have contemplated the beauty, hiddenness, and majesty of the holy. This personal experience of God is essential.

Personal experience, however, is not enough. Not only is my consciousness partial and my understanding incomplete, but the very things I lack may be carried for me in a time-tested and deep religious tradition. My encounter with an authentic religious tradition and its community allows me to test myself by wisdom greater than my own.

This experience of God is not a disembodied one; it rarely exists outside of particular spiritual traditions. Scratch through the surface of any one person's spiritual experience, and you find multiple influences from early religious experience, reading, and even generalized religious norms floating at large in the culture. Most people who pursue a generic spirituality are actually living with multiple religious influences; they just don't know it. In addition, subjective experience may somehow be distorted or partial. No one person holds all the truth; depending on subjective experience alone is not enough.

A living religious tradition carries a particular spiritual path that has been tried, tested, and transmitted over time. When you stand in the midst of a living tradition, you find markers of the path, particular spiritual convictions and suggested practices leading to a fuller, richer, and more faithful life. This path reflects not the insights of one person over the course of one lifetime, but rather centuries of spiritual experience and reflection on it. When a tradition does not fall into the trap of worshiping its own form, but rather the truth to which that form leads, it becomes life-giving.

An authentic spiritual life has a raging conversation with a living tradition–listening to it, arguing with it, taking issue with it, but also finding solace and wisdom in it.

There is no "pure" spirituality, unaffected by traditions. People have longings, intimations, movements of the spirit that lead to a path; but they do not constitute the path itself. Curiosity is not the path, though curiosity is good. And the belief that I have all the truth alone, here in my splendid individuality, free from all the experience of millions throughout history, is a fiction.

Everything in life has form, and this is true of the ways in which our spirituality is embodied. A robust religious life simply recognizes the form of human response to and adoration of the divine. The purpose of the form is to move us beyond, to the formless depth of God, and that, for Christians, becomes freedom in the Spirit.

Do I Have to Limit Myself to One Path?

You will never know what spiritual riches can be found apart from following a particular path. Finding spiritual riches will take time, experimentation, and patience. But the answers you seek will not be forthcoming unless you commit for the long haul. When you find the path that is yours, or when it finds you, give yourself to it. Practice it even when it becomes ordinary, unglamorous, and routine. It doesn't have to give you an adrenaline surge for it to be true. Follow it into the difficult areas, the uncomfortable places. Let it confront your assumptions about yourself and the universe.

Particular paths lead to particular ends. The Christian path is a way that leads to certain places, just as the Buddhist or Muslim path might lead to other end points. If, for example, one practices Zen Buddhism, that path will hopefully lead to enlightenment. The Christian path, on the other hand, leads to an understanding of salvation. These are two different paths leading to two different ends. They may or may not be complementary, but they *are* different. In short, all religious paths are different, though there may be one ultimate reality to which they lead and in which we all rest. If only one reality of God, of the universe, and the cosmos exists, then these different religious paths lead to a particular way of knowing and living in that one reality.

I want to encourage you to take the risk: plunge headlong into the Christian way, its thought and practices, and allow it to take you toward God.

If I Choose to Follow One, What Does That Say about All the Others?

To love your own mother is not to hold disdain for all other mothers. To love your own mother does not even require you to know all the other mothers of the world. You may follow the distinct Christian path without discounting every other way to God. Why? Because you are not in control of the rest of the world or the way God will move in it. Your job is not to stand in judgment of every other religious pathway; that is the province of God only. And because Christians understand that God loves every created being, we believe that God is at work with those of other religious traditions in ways we cannot see or understand. For us, Christ reveals the depth of that love.

Therefore, you are not required to first dismiss every other religion before you decide to take up the Christian faith. Neither must you judge your own path by every other. Rather, make truth claims about what you know. The practice of the Christian faith will rise or fall by its own merits, its own vitality and strength. So free yourself from a fear of either judging others too harshly or not having done your comparative homework sufficiently.

If you want to discover if Christian truth claims actually hold water, then you will have to *live inside them*—a risky proposition, to be sure. To not explore the life of faith from the inside out is like making a decision to buy a house based on curb appeal alone. You haven't taken time to see if the basement leaks during floods or if the dimensions of the bedroom will really accommodate all your furniture. As long as you remain a religious tourist, traveling like an outsider and never really knowing the inside of the places you visit, you will never find your path.

More than that, the Christian faith makes an outlandish claim, one that has been described as foolishness from the very beginning. The Christian message of faith claims not only that God is eternal and present everywhere but also that God acts in particular moments and in particular places. Some have called this the scandal of particularity. This idea might be considered scandalous because the eternal God could never be reduced to such particular coordinates. Christians claim that God entered history, rose up in history, in a specific place and time in order to speak a particular word.

Another way Christians have talked about this particularity is through the word *incarnation.* The idea is a deep one: the awesome holiness of God reveals itself in finite, concrete terms— human terms. Or as the gospel of John puts it, the eternal word, the mediating wisdom of God, becomes flesh, that is, human. We Christians have the reality of God in translated terms.

The most elaborate computer network in the world is of no use to anyone unless it is vetted through particular terminals. The server must have an onramp. I have to have a piece of software, a browser, to connect to what's there; or else the network, as beautiful as it may be, is inaccessible. That's part of what Christians mean when they say God reveals in a particular way, in finite time and space. The Network may be eternal, but I need a modem to connect me.

The revelation of Jesus of Nazareth, in a particular time and place, is just that modem. This revelation of God in time and place includes the whole life of Jesus, his teachings and actions, and eventually the end to which his love leads him. By his resurrection, Christians say, the bridge to the eternal is completed, and you and I are connected by knowing and living in that same power.

Whatever else you believe about God in general, as a Christian you will need to claim some particular things about how God acts in Christ. These claims are the stumbling block over which many fall. In the end, that stumbling block will make a special claim on your life.

How Does That Particularity Translate to Here and Now?

So what does that particular revelation of God have to do with me? How can that make any difference? How do the words of a first-century prophet halfway around the world have an impact now? And how can the death of one man two thousand years ago affect me?

Ah, the relevance question.

One of the principles of the old science, of a rationalistic, materialistic understanding of the universe, was that everything was reduced and subdivided to measurable bits. What you see is what you get. Anything that is not quantifiable cannot exist. Nothing exists beyond the observable, natural world. And along with the old science came the inevitable impact on historic religious claims: God's revealing in time and space could not really exist; no forces beyond history could shape history; no forces beyond nature could affect nature. In other words, the world by necessity had to be cleansed of anything beyond the natural, anything supernatural (above or beyond the natural). Nothing could exist that was super-measurable (beyond the observable and quantifiable). The only things that could survive this static view of the world, as reflected in the writings of those in the Enlightenment, were ideas and nature. God could somehow be present in universal principles or in the design of the natural world.

So what was a stumbling block for the first-century Greco-Roman world, the word about a God acting in a particular time and place, an act that had a universal and lasting impact, became a huge stumbling block for the rationalistic children of the Enlightenment.

Enter Albert Einstein. Enter the new physics. Enter quantum mechanics and string theory. Enter a totally new way to envision the web of forces that connect and shape the universe. Suddenly the old science and its assumptions seem as outdated as the flat world, as the sun revolving around the Earth.

Instead of a static, cause-and-effect world, we now have a webbed universe where everything is connected to everything else, where there is a dramatic continuum of space and time, where the most important things are *not* seen. From the microworld of quarks to the macroworld of huge, galactic fields of energy, the most powerful forces determining human lives are invisible.

Most dramatically, the relation of place to place and the time coordinates of past-present-future have been totally redefined. For instance, physicists have conducted experiments to demonstrate that electrons are paired as twins, paired couples that can exist in a space altogether separate from one another. And yet they are still connected in a parallel way. Join to this the relativity of time—actually affected by velocity moving through space—and a remarkable, paradoxical picture begins to emerge.

What this means, strangely and ironically, is that we have encouragement through the new science to reclaim one of the ancient ways of comprehension: here is there and now is then. In their own way, this is how the ancients considered their own world. Every action of history generated its enduring ripples. A direct web connects both time and place. And a strange, powerful, unknown world lies beyond the seen and sensed one. Unimaginable powers are at work.

When God acts in one place, it has impact everywhere. If something occurs in one phase of time, it is also happening now and has simultaneously affected the future. In fact, it is occurring in the future even as it happens. The present *is* the future. Beyond the limits of perception (time may only be an idea, a passing of events that we experience in a certain kind of way) is God's untime, where what we perceive as a thousand years might be God's day, and there may be no such thing at all as the linear progression of time, only an everywhere-always.

And so, in the fullness of time, in the right place, God acts in a particular way, in the figure of Jesus, in a relatively unknown place in the world; and the impact is known right here and right now.

When the Christian community remembers the story of Jesus healing a man born blind, or listens to one of his stories about an invisible but powerful kingdom of God as small as a mustard seed, or recounts the way his devotion and love led to a martyr's death, we are there, and it is happening now. When he says from the cross, "Father, forgive them, for they don't know what they are doing," we hear that as a word to us, here and now. When we hear his words to the cripple who can now walk, saying, "Get up and walk, your faith has made you well," we start to walk again. Now.

For Further Reflection

Psalm 8	The majesty of God and place of humanity
Genesis 1:1–2, 26–28	A creation story
Exodus 20:1–17	The gift of the law
Romans 3:21–22	Righteousness revealed through faith
James 1:22–25	Faith validated by action
Matthew 12:33–35	The evidence of faith
Mark 12:28–31	The greatest commandments
1 Corinthians 13:1–13	The highest way of love
1 John 4:7–12	Love comes from God
John 14:1–7; 15:1–5	Dwelling place and source
1 Corinthians 1:18–25	The foolishness of the cross
1 Peter 2:4–8	Christ the stumbling block
John 1:1–5, 14	The Word of God revealed
Matthew 16:15–17	The good confession
1 Corinthians 15:1–11	The good news

Jesus the Foundation

At the root of Christianity is Jesus himself, and at the root of Jesus is the reality of God. Everything else is a reflection of or commentary on what God was doing in his life. As you can see, the starting place is *not* the church. In fact, we Christians do not proclaim the church, but the church proclaims Jesus. If you want to talk about first terms, the stuff that makes the real difference, don't start with the church, its history, or the way we have or have not actualized the faith. That's the second term, and it's not the place you start. The community of faith is important, but it is derivative of and flows from the word about Jesus himself.

The Proclamation of Jesus

Jesus was a first-century, spirit-filled Jewish prophet, teacher, and healer obsessed with God's immanent invasion. In fact, the first words out of Jesus' mouth in Mark's gospel, setting the stage for his whole message and ministry were, "The time is fulfilled, and the kingdom of God has come near; repent, and believe in the good news" (Mk. 1:14). In other words, it's all coming down, and you'd better be ready. So what is all the good news about?

To understand the core message of Jesus, you have to under-stand what he called the kingdom or realm or reign or empire of

God, what the Greek New Testament calls the *basileia* of God. The Hebrew word behind the Greek is *malkuth.* In Jesus' native tongue of Aramaic it was *malkuta.* They all have to do with the universe being the sacred network of God.

On the most basic level the reign of God has to do with what is *not* in charge: Everything we normally associate with the power and governance of this world is not, in the end, in charge of anything. The powers of this world are merely clutching at control. Empires and civilizations come and go like seasons of corn. Emperors, presidents, and nations all pass away. But the dynamic energy of God that created and creates, that moves in the world and speaks to hearts is what really holds the cards. This power trumps all earthly powers and in the end, though it may be hidden and show itself in the most unexpected places, it takes the field.

That's why speaking of God's kingdom or reign was and is such a highly charged activity. When you speak of the one reign of God triumphing over all others, you are, at the same time, commenting on all the lesser powers in your life or society or world. You are saying that all these pseudo-kingdoms do not hold the key to the future, understand the world as it might become, or have any real shelf life. What vitality they have is over before it begins. What really matters is the eternal reign of God. And that's the only thing that should demand any ultimate allegiance from us. Of course, that is what the whole idolatry thing is all about. We never allow something less than God to masquerade as though it is God. Only God commands that position. And conversation about the reign of God makes that crystal clear.

Jesus gets at this reign of God primarily through the telling of short, pithy stories called parables. They are found all through the first three canonical gospels (Matthew, Mark, and Luke) commonly referred to as the synoptic gospels. They are also found in some of the early noncanonical Christian collections of the sayings of Jesus such the gospel of Thomas. These stories of Jesus remind us as Christians to stay alert and awake, for one never knows when the master shall return home after a long trip. Banquets are offered where the inconvenienced and hesitant are left outside and those on the edge of society who know their need are invited in. Enemies become heroes as they stop to help the beaten man by the side of the road. Tiny, good-for-nothing mustard seeds are such small and inconsequential signs of the kingdom one might miss them. The joy one has in stumbling over the realm of God is like the joy of finding a hidden treasure or a rare pearl. And the reign of God is embraced with the joy of a woman finding a lost coin, a shepherd finding a lost sheep, and a father finding a lost son.

This reign is here among us, within us, but also on the way to being fulfilled completely. It's something we discover and receive more than own or make. We may not be the authors of this mystery of God-in-the-world, but by faith we can choose to participate and be a part of it.

This reign is the reality toward which Jesus points. In the case of Jesus, the messenger became so identified with the message that he was understood as more than the harbinger of God's realm; he became the premier inhabitant of it. The one who came to proclaim the kingdom came to be proclaimed too; the storyteller became the story. That's what Christians say today. We say that Jesus was the sign for the inbreaking of God's reign. Jesus preached this empire of God, and God made him the sign of it. So when Christians consider Jesus, he is more than teacher and preacher, though he is that. He is the One in whom God acted and is acting.

When the first generation of Christians tried to express just what Jesus meant for them, they reached for titles and metaphors that somehow caught the meaning of his life. Of course, they reached into the only bag they had, the bag of their tradition, symbols, and experience. That's what we have received through the New Testament, the collection of their testimony, witness, and confession of faith. By reading and interpreting their descriptions of Jesus, we are pointed toward that same reality in our lives. And Christians today are faced with the same work: trying to translate our experience of God's mysterious presence into meaningful terms our culture might understand.

Multitudes of titles for Jesus appear in the New Testament. Though they are all honorific in nature, conferring importance and significance, each one has a history and its own connotations in the context in which it is written. Just consider a few:

Christ: This comes from the Greek *Christos*, which in turn came from the Hebrew *messiah*, meaning "anointed one." Prophets and kings were anointed as a sign of holy designation. Christians appropriated this title to communicate the exalted status of Jesus as the anointed one of God, set apart for a special purpose. In time, the title became part of a proper name: Jesus Christ, or Jesus the anointed one. ■

Lord: Though the background of this title begins in Hebrew and is one of the names of God, *Adonai*, the Christian use of the word in Greek, *Kyrios*, has double meanings. To proclaim Jesus as Lord is not only to identify him with God, but also to proclaim that Jesus is the only *Kyrios* who stands above all earthly rulers, even above the Roman Caesars. In the Roman Empire in the time of Jesus rulers were addressed with the same title. As the quintessential protest, Christians said only one Lord of heaven and earth deserves their ultimate loyalty, only one *Kyrios* before whom every knee shall bow, namely the risen Christ. ■

Savior: The Greek word *soter* was used to confer the divine and earthly power to save: to deliver one from physical peril, but also to deliver one from everything that destroys communion with God. The Risen One has become the Savior, the early Christians said, and he saves in many ways. We are saved from our sheer ignorance of God. We are saved from a life apart from God. We are saved from our own self-centered and self-serving inclinations called sin. So, we say, Jesus is the source of our saving, of our salvation. Jesus saves us from a life without Jesus, and therefore provides everything God brings to us through Jesus. ■

Son of Man: In all sources for the life of Jesus, this title is the one Jesus most used in referring to himself. What it means and how he meant it, however, are a little more complex. In Hebrew, people commonly used the phrase "the son of" to connote *belonging-to*. The possessive form, *son of,* in Aramaic was *bar*. Simon *bar* Jonah was Simon son of Jonah. To refer to Jesus *bar* man, Jesus son of man, meant something like *Jesus who belongs to humanity*. The phrase *son of man* is found primarily in Jesus' native tongue of Aramaic and roughly meant "a human being such as myself." This Aramaic phrase, in turn, was translated into the language of the gospels, Koine Greek. This self-reference of Jesus for himself points to the humanity of Jesus, of one who is close to the ground, whose feet get dirty, whose love sends him to the least of these.

The New Testament offers another use of the Son of Man sayings. This use is called the apocalyptic one. In the literature between the Old and New Testaments, in the time immediately preceding and following Jesus, a strong expectation arose among many that God would bring history to a close in a cataclysmic way. Allusions to this occur in the Old Testament book of Daniel (7:13–14) with its references to the Son of Man and in the inter-testamental material (between the testaments) in the books of Enoch and also in portions of the gospels, the early letters of Paul, and the Revelation of John.

All of these look forward to an immanent close of history brought about by God. The figure of the Son of Man was identified with this future, and Jesus refers to this figure in one of his parables that refers to the Son of Man as the one who would come (Mt. 25:31). Later, following the resurrection, Christians began to combine their future expectation of the close of history and the coming of the Son of Man with the risen Jesus himself. So the church developed an understanding that the risen Christ would himself appear at the close of history. This understanding was a statement of faith about God and God in Christ. Though later Christian witnesses spoke of Jesus in these terms, he did not, in the earliest record, speak of himself in those terms. ■

Son of God: This title is perhaps the one most used in naming the peculiar relationship of Jesus to his God. Like the son of man title, it connotes belonging: the son of God belongs to God, as a child belongs to and is an extension of the parent. In the New

Testament witness, however, this title reflects a good deal more than that.

The Son of God title is not broadly used in Judaism. It rather emerges more directly out of the first-century Greco-Roman traditions of the divine man. Many so-called divine persons emerged during that time, often living in a transient state, moving about teaching, gathering a following, and performing wonders. But the witnesses of the New Testament make a special claim about Jesus: this man is specifically designated and set apart by God, sent for a redemptive purpose to the world. This status, this role, this designation will be recognized by those to whom it has been revealed. In dramatic biblical narratives, the demons are the first to know who he is, as their livelihood is placed in jeopardy by his very presence. ■

Later Christians, upon reflecting on the unique sonship of Jesus, spun out this relationship in more metaphysical terms. If Jesus, the Son, is a part of God, then the whole reality of God must contain his sonship. Out of this idea and the need to clearly place Jesus in direct relation to God, the doctrine of the *trinity* emerged: one reality of God (not several gods) that is thoroughly relational, a unity that is diverse. In the gospel of John this relationality is expanded to its grand conclusion. The eternal Son preexists the earthly Jesus and postexists him too. As a mystery, God takes on human flesh and dwells among humans in this concrete life. As another mystery, the sent One returns to the eternity of God, enlivening Christians' faith and trust as he goes.

Christians differ on how they approach Jesus and how they allow him to approach them. Some see him as God's man, the earthy prophet, an outbreak of the Spirit in human flesh. Others have a higher, more exalted understanding of the risen, reigning Christ. For both poles of this continuum, the title Son of God speaks to that mysterious figure of Jesus who, through faith, becomes the Christ for us.

However you find yourself encountering Jesus, you will most likely find yourself either being attracted or repulsed. People tend to have one reaction or the other. Like magnetism, the positive or negative polls can either push or pull objects toward them. That being the case, an authentic encounter with Jesus from any vantage point or approach often places you in a kind of crisis of the soul, a spiritual dilemma. Unless that mysterious One is just dismissed from consciousness so as to avoid dealing with him, he will, by his very nature, call for a decision.

The apostle Paul described this by saying that Jesus tends to offend everyone; whatever your preconceived notions, he is going to confound them. He scandalizes you, upsets your tidy or untidy world. If you expect one thing, he will deliver another. He even goes so far as to say that the Christian proclamation appears weak and foolish to any and all comers. This is no self-help manual for spiritual growth. No, Christ becomes a stumbling block, something that trips you up and sends you careening one way or the other. In the end, after you've stubbed your toe and lunged headlong toward the pavement, what seemed to be foolishness becomes God's wisdom, God's way of undermining all of your little intellectual constructions, your way of looking at the world, your politics.

This stumbling block is one of the primary reasons so many people turn aside from Jesus. I would guess it's exactly the case with you too. That encounter puts you in the horns of a dilemma, doesn't it? Once you come face-to-face with this Jesus, you're going to have make some decisions. In the middle of those decisions you will find that the most elemental choices are required of you. Saying yes to this revelation of God means saying no to so many other things in your life.

In the end, you can only know whether the Christian way works by following it. This course is different from studying it from a safe academic distance, objectively comparing it to all comers or attempting to explore it from outside an actual Christian community. This sanitary effort never works because it never dares to get inside the story; it is always an outside job. Without actually getting on the path and walking it, you'll never find where it leads. That's true of almost anything in life, but it's doubly true of the Christian faith. It's risky, I know, but can you think of one thing of great value that is not?

For Further Reflection

Mark 1:14–15   The proclamation of Jesus

Some Parables of Jesus

Mark 2:21–22 (Mt. 9:16–17; Lk. 5:36–38; *Thomas* 47)
Wineskins

Mark 4:3–8 (Mt. 13:3–8; Lk. 8:5–8; *Thomas* 9a)
The sower

Mark 4:26–29
The seed

Mark 4:30–32 (Mt. 13:31–32; Lk. 13:18–19; *Thomas* 20)
The mustard seed

Mark 12:1–9 (Mt. 21:33–41; Lk. 20:9–16; *Thomas* 65a)
The son and the vineyard

Matthew 13:33 (Lk. 13:20–21; *Thomas* 96)
The yeast

Matthew 22:1–4 (Lk. 14:16–24; *Thomas* 64a)
The wedding banquet

Matthew 13:24–30 (*Thomas* 57)
The wheat and the weeds

Matthew 13:44 (*Thomas* 109)
The treasure in the field

Matthew 13:45–46 (*Thomas* 76a)
The pearl of great price

Matthew 18:12–13 (Lk. 15:4–6; *Thomas* 107)
The lost sheep

Matthew 18:23–34
The ungrateful servant

Matthew 20:1–15
The laborers in the vineyard

Matthew 25:1–12
The ten bridesmaids

Matthew 25:14–30 (Lk. 19:11–27)
The talents

Luke 10:30–35
The good Samaritan

Luke 12:16–20 (*Thomas* 63a)
The barns

Luke 13:6–9
The fig tree

Luke 14:28–30
The tower

Luke 14:31–32
Counting the cost

Luke 15:8–9
The lost coin

Luke 15:11–32
The waiting father

Luke 18:2–5
The widow's faith

Luke 18:10–13
The Pharisee and the tax collector

Taking the Plunge

By this time you may be asking, How do you actually become a Christian? What steps do you take? How do you know if you are ready? Is there a minimum of knowledge required to take the first step? Is it more a matter of head or heart?

Receive and Love

Because we believe that the One who created us is always coming after us first, our starting point is not with our own actions, but rather with the grand story of God, the first actor. The good news is that God initiates a relationship, and we rejoice in being found when we could not find. The love of this God is not contingent on certain preconditions or worthiness on our part.

Because the nature of the God we know in Christ is love and because love always reaches out to the beloved, we are the most sought after beings in the world. God desires nothing more than we accept the love offered. Whereas a life without a connection to the main power of the universe is estranged and alienated, our loving God majors in loving the unlovable just to make a point: real love embraces in spite of the condition of the beloved. We call this *grace*.

Respond and Follow

A dynamic relationship, though, is completed when it flows two ways. That's what faith is about. Faith is our response to the graceful embrace of God. It is receiving the gift and then loving God in return. In other words, once you are awakened to the mystery of the elegant, spacious, and connected energy of the cosmos and your place in it, the natural response is one of wonder, awe, gratitude, and love.

Think of it this way: When the disciples of Jesus just picked up and followed him, they did so without fully knowing why. They left their old lives and headed toward new ones before they knew exactly who they were following. They knew enough to begin the journey even though much more was yet to be revealed. They were first caught by the love of God, and then they tried to understand it and, more importantly, to live it.

You and I come to faith the same way. Somehow in the strange timetable of the Spirit, we are caught by a mystery that is far beyond us. In the face of Christ we see a reflection of eternity that calls our name. Through a host of witnesses past and present we are pointed toward the horizon of God. But because we will never exhaust the mystery of God and because our understanding is limited, we must begin the journey before all the questions are answered. The point is that our hearts have been called by love, and we follow it as moths to the flame.

Believe and Declare

Soon enough, the disciples of Jesus came to a turning point. They all headed off to a place away from the crowds, and then in a quiet time apart they came face-to-face with the deepest questions of their lives. The questions probed the identity of Jesus and what they would do with him and become with him.

First, Jesus asked his disciples to report on the word from the street: What do people say about me? The report is favorable: He might be one of the prophets, perhaps like John the Baptist, or even the coming messianic figure Elijah. All these tributes are positive ones, casting Jesus in an admirable light. But they do not really hit the mark.

The word on the street today might be a similar one. Who is Jesus? A wise teacher, perhaps? A holy man or prophet? One of the great spiritual leaders? Jesus might receive high marks in today's culture, even though most people don't really know what he is about. For many in our culture Jesus is the product of sentimentality, the Jesus of the consumer culture holidays of Christmas and Easter. Or he is one of the popularized versions of our own creation, a new action hero or mystical sage. Who is this Jesus, really? And what in the world is God doing through him?

Before they knew it, Jesus turned the whole inquiry process directly toward his disciples. Now the question is not in the form of a poll taken from the street but rather a sounding of the disciples themselves: So, who do *you* say that I am? Now it gets personal.

That's the question that comes to you and me, Who do *you* say that he is? Not what your brother or the artist or cutlery salesperson thinks, but rather what *you* believe. This personal question moves us from the realm of intellectual curiosity to the place of deep faith, from exterior analysis to interior apprehension.

The alpha disciple, Simon, steps forward and takes a deep breath: "You are the Messiah, the Son of the living God" (Mt. 16:16). Those words have become the central confession of the Christian community ever since, what we affectionately call the good confession.

To make this confession is to say that Jesus was the one sent and anointed by God to bring as much of God to us as we could possibly stand. Your confession is exactly that, y*our* confession, not a consensus of the crowd. This *I* believe. This confession is the foundation on which everything else is based. It stands as the beginning point in the move from following in curiosity to believing in trust. This confession is the only one Christians expect as one joins the company of those who have believed and said the same. The rest of your life will be spent unpacking all of the implications of that deep, deep confession.

In response to Simon's statement Jesus makes three statements. First, he says no person revealed this confession to Simon. Rather, such knowledge comes from the Spirit. When you come to faith, when you are drawn to the Jesus who is the Christ, it is because God has moved you that way. Second, he gives Simon a new name. Renaming was especially important in the Jewish tradition. A new name reflects the transformation that has taken place. He said Simon was to become Peter, which in Greek means "rock." The meaning of the new name is simple: He may not have become a rock star, but he sure did become *rock man.* And on this rock Jesus would create his beloved community. Not even the most hellish powers would be able tear it apart. After all, the beloved community is built on nothing less than the faith of the rock man, Peter. Third, Jesus says that Peter gets a new set of keys. But these are not the same car keys you receive when you turn sixteen. These are the keys that open the lock of the reign of God. Peter's trusting faith has become a rock on which the beloved community stands and lives into the real empire and reign and realm of God. This spiritual power unlocks things. This spiritual power has authority. In a sense, every Christian, standing on the same rock of Peter, is a part of that same key chain. More than anything, the Christian does not derive spiritual power from herself, but rather from the One who gives the keys. This is what we mean when we say the church is *apostolic*–it derives its authority and mission from this keystone of the apostles.

Wet and Wild

What we discover through the various authors of the New Testament is that baptism is the symbolic way in which Christians dramatize new life in Christ.

In one sense Christian baptism is reminiscent of earlier Jewish practices of ritual purification, such as the practices of John the Baptizer, the cousin of Jesus. Jesus himself received John's baptism as he came to fulfill his destiny and calling. The message of the gospel writers is clear: When Jesus wades into this river, he crosses over into his public ministry. He carries his identity as God's Son and possesses a special measure of the Spirit.

As we walk the way of Jesus, we eventually recognize a time to turn around and head toward God. The waters of baptism become mighty waters through which we pass to a new life. We also recognize that in our baptism we possess a name, an identity as children of God and the always-accompanying Spirit.

In the early stories of Christian baptism people responded to the good news of Christ by confessing their belief and following that with baptism. Baptism usually occurs within the gathered community of the believers, but it is sometimes spontaneous with only a few present. In the Greco-Roman societies of the first century in which the collective was more important than the individual, baptism was sometimes extended to an entire household as they followed the lead of the head of that household.

The apostle Paul had a deeply developed understanding of baptism, one that joins the symbolism of Christ's death and resurrection with plunging under and coming out of the waters. In the same way that Christ died, so we die to our old selves, and in the same way that Christ was raised, so we rise to a new life in Christ: The old is gone and the new has come.

Baptism is an event in the life of the individual believer, to be sure, but it is more than that. A new believer is baptized into the whole body of believers, the body of Christ. A believer becomes one part of the whole of Christ's body, the church. Analogous to the physical body, no part of the body of Christ holds the same function or place as any other part. Each member participates in the one spirit of Christ and builds up the whole body.

Christian baptism is not a rite exclusive to one local congregation; believers are baptized into the body of Christians in all places throughout the entire world. This is what we mean when we refer to the church universal. This is our extended Christian family, and we recognize the baptisms of those who have been baptized in different ways in different traditions.

Growing in Christ

The faithful response to God's grace, followed by baptism, is the beginning of the spiritual journey. As we surrender more and more to God, we move increasingly toward living a holy life. By that we mean a life that is more and more in harmony with the image of God in which we have been created. Day by day the soul grows in spiritual depth as it communes more deeply with the Spirit of Christ.

The Christian life, then, is a life given to God, a life placed in God's hands and put at the disposal of God's purposes. It is not an easy journey or one suited for the fainthearted. Progress is often uneven, and people move forward in different patterns of avoidance and embrace. We resist the persistent pull toward our lower nature that places our own needs and desires over all else, and we strive to reach toward the upward call of God. That upward motion unites the centermost part of life with the source of life. At that juncture, that holy place where a believer's heart meets the heart of God, Christians rest, dwell, and find their peace. It is the place where Christians lose their lives to find their lives.

Of course, to proclaim Jesus as Lord is to simultaneously declare what is not Lord. The baptized life mandates a choosing: between Christ and all that is not consistent with Christ in our personal lives, the church, society, and the world. We measure all values, decisions, and policy by a life lived for God. This choosing includes a critique of what is popular in the culture, held by majority consensus, or legitimated by political power. We worship but one Lord of life, by whom all else is evaluated.

Therefore the body of the church does not merely reflect the values of the society in which it is found. It does not exist to legitimize the actions of its nation or act as a chaplain for one political tribe. Instead, the church is to fulfill its confession and live in the resurrected life. At its most revolutionary, the church lives by a vision of the reign of God, becoming leaven in the world. God calls Christians to be salt in the bland stew of the world and light shining among the shadows of life.

At the centerpoint of the Lordship of Christ, we Christians take courage in our prophetic voice. Here compassion wells up, and injustice is exposed for what it is. We speak, we serve, and we act, not on our own behalf, but rather for the sake of the One who became love, compassion, and justice for us. Through him we become awakened to God's passion for justice and longing for peace. This is not a human project or a matter of one's favorite ideology, but of God's ways that confound all of our own.

When communities of the baptized live out their calling to mission in the world, they act and speak with passion and courage. When the leaders of Christian communities speak at their best, it is not only a matter of opinion, but of faithfully striving to discern the will of God.

Living with a Bigger Story

Why do people who become avid sports fans seldom fail to support their alma mater, attend the holiday parade, or pause to remember those who have gone before? The common connection is clear: They long to be part of something larger than themselves. They want to know that their lives are more than they are primarily by connection to something else. For the sports fan, these activities are connected to a team, the sign of corporate identity. For the alumni the activities are connected to a school, a place that shaped them and they hope shapes others. The parade attendees hope they can join in the drama of life.

These, however important, are not ultimate connections and stories. What people of faith strive to discover is a way of living in which they are swept up in a larger story. The scope is cosmic, the ideals out of reach, and the hope shining and spectacular. Believers dare to say that the God of this elegant, baffling, unfolding cosmos is mysteriously at work, and by God's grace they have knowingly become a part of it.

In the same way that Israel looks back, remembers its deliverance from oppression and bondage in Egypt, and says, When *we* were taken out of Egypt…, so we Christians understand that we are a part of a story of faith that is our own.

For Further Reflection

Romans 5:6–9	God's love for the ungodly
Acts 2:37–42	The response of faith
Romans 6:3–11	Baptism into the death and resurrection of Christ
1 John 4:7–12	God first loved us
Mark 1:9–11	The baptism of Jesus
Mark 1:16–20	Jesus calls disciples
Matthew 16:13–20	The good confession
1 Corinthians 12:12–13	Baptized into the body
2 Corinthians 5:17–20	The new creation
Acts 8:26–38	The baptism of the Ethiopian
Acts 9:1–19	The conversion of Saul (Paul)
Acts 16:13–15	The baptism of Lydia and her household
Matthew 5:13–16	Become salt and light

6

One Is the Loneliest Number[*]

I Am Not My Own; Therefore, I Am.

As important as the concept of freedom is, especially as it regards freedom from tyranny or bondage, few social doctrines have been more misused or misunderstood. When freedom joins with personal selfishness, it is used to authorize any behavior at the expense of any relationship. My freedom is your pain. I do it because I can do it. When freedom joins with national selfishness, it is used to authorize any policy that gives a country what it desires at the expense of any other country. National freedom joined with power becomes another nation's bad news.

This misuse of the concept of freedom is one that Christians must consider seriously; but other aspects of the idea of freedom also hold important sway, especially in the American psyche. They are the twin notions of autonomy and self-reliance.

Two strains of poetry embodying these notions of autonomy and self-reliance are from the British poet William Ernest Henley, and American singer Frank Sinatra. Henley lived in the late 1800s and was a contemporary of such poets as Robert Louis Stevenson. As one who endured much personal suffering due to difficult

---

[*]From "One," lyrics by Harry Nilsson.

51

health, Henley summed up the source of courage in his poem "Invictus." Whatever would come, one thing stood at the end of the day: I am the master of my fate, the captain of my soul. If one song defined the repertoire of Frank Sinatra, it was one song that was requested the most and always brought people to their feet: *My Way.* You may remember the refrain "I did it my way." It is the motto of many.

The Christian life turns these two axioms on their heads.

As we tenaciously cling to the ego, remain preoccupied with the self, and continue to insist that we are the masters of our own destinies as we do it our way, we remain stuck in one of the greatest spiritual problems of our time: Narcissism.

As a counterpoint to that prevailing narcissism, Christ calls Christians to an ever-increasing surrender to God, which means surrendering many of the claims for our lives. The more we let go the more we find. Christians then say the inconceivable: I am a servant to Christ, therefore I am free. I am free from the demands of the ego that keep me from true freedom. I am free from a whole host of wants, concerns, and security needs that dominate my waking hours. I am free from the preoccupation with my death and its related need to control everyone and everything. I am free because I am not my own, but rather belong to Christ. I am free, then, to be Christ for the neighbor, not in splendid isolation, but rather in deeply committed community. And that, in the Christian way of thinking, is perfect freedom. I am not captive to myself, but free to love God and neighbor.

This connected way of life all begins with interrelationships in the life of God. For instance, the wisdom of God manifests itself in the life of Jesus. Jesus is one with the spirit of God. The resurrected Christ sits at the right hand of God. And the Spirit abides with us even in the absence of Jesus. All these aspects of God's movement and being are distinct and yet related to one another. Not only do people perceive God in many modes or forms; these forms are all mysteriously connected. Only one God exists—we are monotheists after all—but many aspects and movements exist within God.

In the evolution of Christian thought, spiritual leaders within the church attempted to define the ways in which God, Christ, and Holy Spirit are all related one to the other. One way they resolved the enigma of these interrelationships was by means of the concept of the Trinity.

You can put your Bible down if you are searching for the word *Trinity*. It isn't there because it developed later in the life of the church and was given its primary form in 325 C.E. by the first ecumenical council of the church in Nicea. The Trinity is a concept that explains how the life of God can be both a unity and plurality at the same time. Simplicity and complexity coexist. Unity and diversity are one. Because the foundation of reality is itself relational, the faithful life is to be lived relationally too. You are not alone. Everything is connected. This connected universe of God shapes the way we live in relationship to God, the world, and the Christian community.

In the World, but Not Owned by It

Because God created and continues to create the entire cosmos and because humans are a part of this intricate web of creation, we treasure and claim the world and all that is within it. In this respect, we are a part of the whole, one with the rest of our universe, one with all created beings, connected through forces visible and invisible.

As those who are utterly dependent on our Creator and interdependent with the whole created order, we regard our world with reverence, respect, and care. In fact, we have a special vocation as stewards of the creation in which we live.

Although we are in solidarity with the whole world, we do not uncritically accept the ways or values of those who are not in conscious relationship with God. We do not automatically accept the worldview of our dominant culture. We live among a created humanity that, in large part, either does not know or misunderstands its creator.

On a scale with total absorption into the world on one end and total withdrawal from the world on the other, Christians find themselves poised in the center, balancing the goodness of creation on the one hand and knowledge of its brokenness on the other. We are in the good world but not owned by it, called to serve our neighbors without automatically appropriating the ways of the culture.

Life in Christian Community

Because we are baptized into the one body of Christ, we are part of a community of believers yoked together with Christ and living in the Spirit. This community of faith is a gift, the extended family of faith sharing a common story, edifying one another, providing witness to the world, and remaining accountable to Christ's calling.

This community of the Spirit is not an optional thing, an association of like-minded people. No, Christians are joined together in a common discipleship to this one we call Lord. We know that through his life, death, and new life with God we have been made his own. We are his people, his royal priesthood.

Because the one spirit apportions many gifts to the body, we find our place in the Christian community by identifying and using our gifts for the building up of the whole body. The mission of the church is composed of those who dare to use their gifts for ministry in the body.

This way of life together is also shaped and nurtured by sharing a common set of spiritual practices. For instance, the ways of prayer, observing the Sabbath, sharing the Lord's Prayer, giving of offerings, and studying scripture are all ingredients that, when shared, foster deep connection, common identity, and mutual love. When Christians come together to celebrate significant life passages such as infant dedications, baptism, and ordinations to ministry, our bonds are strengthened even more. By observing seasons of the church's year, such as Advent or Holy Week, we begin to understand the alternate calendar by which our community lives, one that stands outside of ordinary time.

Defining One and Many

In many cultures it has been and is natural to define oneself according to the group: I am what we are. The tribe offers protection, and my best chance of survival is found there. In many modern Western cultures, on the other hand, the opposite thinking is most prevalent: the community is understood as an assemblage of individuals. Fullness of personhood requires a separation from the herd to be a part of it.

The New Testament understanding of Christian community, however, provides an alternate way to understand the relationship of the one to the many. The Christian way is not based on either sociology or psychology. It is not based on preferences, the gathering of like-minded people, or individual differences. This particular community of the Spirit is formed by persons sharing a distinctive theological understanding. Christian community is neither a group determining the identity of the individual or a constellation of individuals comprising the group. It is a community formed because the same Lord has claimed all of its members and they all live in the same spiritual presence. They draw upon the same story, and as they live in it they become shaped by it.

Covenant and Commitment

As one enters the beloved community by means of baptism, a powerful rite of making a covenant, so a new kind of relationship develops with both God and the community.

The entire sacred story, from its beginning until now, tells of God's initiative in establishing a relationship of loving-kindness, and then the resulting human response to it. The stories of Adam, Abraham, Moses, and Jesus illustrate the ongoing saga of covenant making, a surrender to the One who wants to be our God if we will be God's people. People never make good on their end of the deal, of course, but that does not deter the great Lover. They are brought back, restored, and reconciled to live in the vitality of covenant again.

The connections of covenant extend to brothers and sisters in Christ, too, as we promise to live together in the love of Christ. We are committed to one another not because it is beneficial to do so, but because we are united by sacred promises. Because God reaches to us, we reach to one another; and that is the tie that binds. The covenant means that leaving one another because of difference of opinion is out of the question. It means we are mutually accountable to one another for the commitments we have made. It also means we seriously regard the special call of those within the body who have been vested with leadership. In good faith, we promise to support and pray for them.

Our Ecumenical Life and Vocation

If the love of God has been shown so clearly in Christ, and if that spirit of love has filled our hearts, we become a spirit-formed community in which the love of Christ flows through our spiritual veins and arteries. Such a body is fundamentally one because Christ has made us one. This unity of the church, therefore, is the gift of God that we receive, treasure, and foster. In spite of our human inclination to divide and rupture, the spirit continues to unify.

The term used to describe this form of unity is *ecumenical.* This word is based on the Greek word, *oikoumene*, which means the whole, inhabited world. If Christians and churches act in an ecumenical way, they are recognizing the unity of Christ throughout the cosmos.

The breakdown of ecumenical life is found in the many divisions in the church, past and present. They reveal spiritual illness. They evidence rebellion against God and arrogance toward neighbors. Healing the tears in this fabric requires both a renewed vision for God's unity and our humble willingness to pursue it. If, as one Disciples of Christ founder Thomas Campbell said, "Christian unity is our polar star," then we must be willing to recognize it and pursue it and make it a priority. Christian unity is not one program among many; it is one of the primary marks of the faithful church. Local, national, and global councils of churches are signs of this ecumenical passion for unity. They are not auxiliary to the church, but an expression of the unity Christ gives the whole church.

Jesus prayed for the unity of the faithful (Jn. 17), and we know that God's greatest desire is that we become one, even as Jesus was one with his Father and one with his disciples.

This unity of spirit should not be confused with uniformity; those are two different things. Uniformity defines harmony in terms of sameness; if we are all alike or all agree, then we are unified. In contrast to a model of sameness, deep Christian unity appeals to the love of Christ that underlies all things, especially differences. In fact, true unity is most revealed when it thrives in the presence of diversity. This unity is evidence of the abiding, reconciling love of Christ.

Unity may exist with a multiplicity of historically shaped forms and traditions. That is, many congregations, denominations, and movements may exist in unity. What must be present in the midst of all these diverse forms, however, is a mutual recognition of the faith, ministry, sacraments, and mission of the other. As one body of Christ, we must be willing to see and affirm the presence of the one Lord in the life of the other. As such, we will always strive to draw the body together in joint service, mutual understanding, shared worship, and common witness. We come together not because it is practical or because we are creating unity; we are demonstrating the unity that already exists through Christ.

Christians Worship Together

At the heart of the gathered Christian community is worship–adoring and praising God, preaching and teaching the story of our faith, praying, and the sharing the Lord's Table. In worship the Christian community is most itself and becomes that which it is meant to be.

From the earliest of times, Christians set aside Sunday as their Sabbath, the day on which their Lord rose from the dead. Sunday became their day of devotion and rest. Practicing

Christians keep the Sabbath as one of their foundational disciplines. It is neither optional nor to be determined by the emotions of the moment. It is something offered to God and shared in Christian community in all times. Keeping the Sabbath frees us from the grind of commerce, the compulsion to work, and the illusion that we become greater by doing more. Keeping the Sabbath reminds us that we belong to God and that God is holy. The set apart pause of Sabbath strangely sanctifies all of the other days of the week, putting them in proper perspective.

The form of Christian worship has varied throughout time and place. Though an early form of the liturgy (Gk: *liturgia*, the work of the people) developed through a combination of the Jewish synagogue service (psalms, scripture, and prayer) with a sharing of the Lord's supper, those ingredients have been combined together throughout history in a variety of ways. Through time traditions emerged and grew, and different aspects of worship came to be emphasized more than others. Moves toward more ornamentation were balanced by moves toward more simplicity. The cultural context shaped the way worship was formed and practiced. While some worship in grand cathedrals, others celebrate their common life in small house churches.

The following are important aspects of worship that need to be present regardless of the historic or cultural form: The people gather together in one place; they praise and adore their God who is the object of their worship; they hear the words of scripture faithfully taught and preached; they lift their hearts to God in prayer; and they hold the Lord's supper at the center of worship every Lord's day.

The Table in the Middle

One of the defining characteristics of the ministry of Jesus was his practice of table fellowship with all manner of people. These meal celebrations were occasions for teaching and encountering the most unusual people, those outside the "clean" boundaries of the socially acceptable. Christians understand these meals as a sign of the upside down nature of God's reign, one that turns over our own sense of propriety.

At the close of his life, as he faced his own death, Jesus gathered his disciples in for a Passover meal. As they celebrated the story of the great deliverance of Israel from the clutches of burden and oppression, Jesus added new meaning and symbolism to that meal. From then on, anytime they broke the bread and shared the cup they would remember that, like the broken bread, his life was broken for them, and, like the crushed grape, so his life was crushed in order that his blood would be a sign of the faithful love of God. They would do this in remembrance of him, and by remembering, the past would become present. This Jesus meal would look forward to the ever-approaching reign of God, in which the faithful would sit at table with all those who loved God throughout time and eternity. In this sense, the supper is a foretaste of the greater banquet yet to come.

The letters of the apostle Paul provide a glimpse into the sharing of the Lord's table in the earliest Christian communities. Paul passed on the tradition of the table that he had received, including the words of institution Christians recite at the table to this day: "For I received from the Lord what I also handed on to you, that the Lord Jesus…" (1 Cor. 11:23). He also offers words of correction to the Christian community, counseling them on the proper way to observe the meal. They are to show remarkable concern for all persons in the church, especially those from lower stations in life. They examine themselves and partake in a worthy manner, so that the outer rite is matched with an earnest and sincere inner intention.

In the earliest record of the church Christians celebrated at the Lord's table every time they gathered to worship. So this meal stands at the center of Christian worship and indeed shapes the way the church understands itself as a part of the reign of God. As a reflection of the radically inclusive table fellowship of Jesus, the supper is extended to all who would come to Christ and sup. He invites, and those who preside are merely stand-ins, humble servants offering a gracious invitation on his behalf. Christ does not invite only those who are members of the Disciples of Christ community, but all Christians, regardless of their denominational affiliation.

In the Disciples of Christ tradition, the ordained and lay elders most often preside at the table together, representing the ministry of the whole church. This familiar combination of lay and ordained table leadership connects in two ways. The ordained provide continuity with the apostolic and universal church, and lay elders provide connection with the ministry of the baptized.

The Universal and Future Table

First, we recognize one Lord, one faith, one baptism, and one table of the Lord that we share in the whole inhabited world, and one future into which God calls us. Then the conclusion is undeniable: The unity celebrated now at the table is not a fully realized one. It is but a foretaste of the full and complete banquet of God's people to come, the ultimate love feast. The Christian hope is that God will gather us in from north, south, east, and west to share with that cloud of witnesses that surrounds us even now.

We already have a taste of it, of course. We smell the bread baking in the oven. Its fragrance wafts through the house and fills us with great anticipation. How is this possible? Because now is then, and here is there. And God is in the middle of it all. What a life!

For Further Reflection

Matthew 16:24–26	Losing your life to find your life
(Mk. 8:34–38; Lk. 9:23–27)	
Romans 1:1	Becoming a servant to Christ
1 Corinthians 1:30	Christ, the wisdom of God
John 1:14	The Word of God becomes flesh
John 14:18–21, 25–27	Living in God through Christ in the power of the Holy Spirit
Genesis 1:26	Serving as stewards of creation

1 Peter 2:9	We are a royal priesthood, living in God's light
1 Corinthians 12:4–27	Finding your spiritual gifts in the body of Christ
2 Corinthians 5:17–19	Becoming agents of God's reconciliation
John 17:20–22	Jesus' prayer that his disciples all become one
Acts 2:42	The church centering its life in worship
Luke 22:19–20	Jesus shares the last supper with his disciples
1 Corinthians 11:23–26	The early community shares the table

Moving in, Moving out

The energy pattern of the Christian life is like an oscillating inward and outward motion. The Spirit creates a kind of centripetal force, a center-seeking force, that holds itself in a balance with our outward velocity. Without that center of gravity we would be cast wildly off to the outer boundaries. Without outward motion we would collapse in on ourselves. The balance between the two is what makes it dynamic.

To achieve such balance in the Christian life requires much more than holding certain convictions; it requires a way of life, spiritual practices that shape the person, and community from generation to generation.

And on the Seventh Day…

The cornerstone spiritual practice of the Christian life is borrowed from Judaism: the keeping of the Sabbath. In one of the creation stories from the book of Genesis, on the seventh day God enters a deep rest from the labor of creating. This, then, becomes the model for balancing the life of rest and labor, outward action and inward reflection, personal striving and Godly focus. At least once a week the faithful person is to put aside the life of commerce—buying and selling, working, justifying life by what one does—and instead keep the quiet rest of God.

Keeping the Sabbath, then, becomes the archetypal model for the entire life of faith.

Christians modified the day on which the Sabbath was observed in Judaism (Friday sundown to Saturday sundown) by setting aside the first day of the week, Sunday, the day on which the Lord rose from the dead. Beginning with sundown on Saturday evening and continuing through the day of Sunday, Christians set aside the day for God. This day includes worship with other Christians, quiet reflection and inspiration, collective worship, time to nourish the soul with friends and family, and rest. Though Christians strive to not work on the Sabbath by arrangement with their employers, it sometimes becomes impossible. Those Christians who have no choice but to work on the Sabbath seek out alternative ways to set aside time for the Spirit.

As one continues to practice keeping the Sabbath, other things become internalized as well. The first and most obvious is overcoming the compulsion to do, earn, and perform. The meaning of life is not to be found in earning a place in the universe, but rather in accepting the graciousness of God. Being still before God, as one receiving the gift, makes the other six days holy.

Being still before God, bringing the heart to rest, is the beginning of the prayerful life. The focus of attention is redirected to the eternal quality of life and to one's deep dependence on God. And the regular keeping of the Sabbath shapes one's whole perspective on life in deep and lasting ways. Setting aside time for a holy purpose transfers into other spiritual practices as well.

Lord, Teach Us How to Pray

As Christians pursue the lifelong path of discipleship, they learn to set aside time every day to nurture the way of the spirit. This often includes finding a simple prayer discipline, through trial and error, that is most effective for the individual.

Many Christians set aside a determined time of the morning or evening for a quiet time with God. During this time one may engage in spiritual reading of a devotional classic or current inspirational work, slowly read and pray the Psalms, meditate on short sections of scripture, or lift out portions of those scriptures for more extended meditation and reflection.

A time-honored prayer practice for Christians, known as early as the second century, is praying the Lord's Prayer twice a day upon rising and going to sleep. This practice frames the day with the prayer Jesus taught his disciples.

The traditional fivefold pattern of verbal or mental prayer is often a useful pattern to guide one's prayer: praise, thanksgiving, forgiveness, intercession (prayer for others), and petition (prayer for self).

One may devotionally read the ancient or modern prayers of others and allow them to speak to God in ways not quite accessible to oneself.

In spiritual formation, individual differences are important; people pray differently, and different prayer practices speak to some more than others. Highly kinesthetic people need movement to join body and soul. They may need to think and pray while walking. Others may meditate more completely with their hands occupied in a repetitive task. Others may pray more deeply while singing the prayer or painting the feeling. A labyrinth walk may best serve the needs of some while another may best pray by gazing upon a candle or icon. The more solitary person needs to be absolutely alone while the more outward person gives and receives energy through shared prayer and the closeness of others.

Prayer retreats, either solitary retreats or group retreats, are indispensable for the cultivation of the spirit. Many people set aside regular times for prayer and meditation getaways to a quiet place—a retreat center, cabin, or monastery—to step out of the grind of life into the quiet of God. These times may be relatively short (twenty-four hours) or longer, such as a week. Some find a helpful balance in a guided retreat with others that provides solitary time as well. Silent retreats often drive one into the quiet places of the soul that have been covered over by outer and inner noise.

Many do not naturally have access to some of the deepest sort of prayer, the contemplative forms of deep silence and the way of practicing the Presence without words. This prayer comes, if it does at all, with long periods of wordless waiting upon the presence of God. The goal is deep communion with God, a losing of oneself in the beauty, depth, and mystery of God.

If you are a person with small children, a busy family, or a demanding career, you may need to develop the fine art of short conversations with God—outbursts, if you will. Your time may be found during the morning drive to work or with that sandwich between meetings or during the baby's naptime. Short sentence prayers repeated at intervals throughout the day whenever the time presents itself may become the lingua franca of your prayer life. You may have heard a compelling verse of scripture during your Sabbath worship, and you latch onto it as your prayer petition of the week: *Lord, place my feet upon the rock.* These sentence prayers will keep your mind centered on the glory of God, an island in the storm. Or you may pray spontaneously as needs present themselves, as the ambulance passes by, as the news of grim tragedy sounds on your radio, or as your child shares one of the struggles of growing up. These are all opportunities to practice a prayerful life in which everything is offered up to God.

Underlying all spiritual longings and practices is an abiding knowledge that the Spirit speaks when we cannot, that God allows us to respond when we feel powerless, and that even when we are having a terrible time tuning in to God, God still makes it possible.

Prayer, in the end, is a gift of the Spirit. When we allow Spirit winds to blow through us, there comes a deep connection to the core of the universe of which we are all a part.

Where Your Treasure Is...

If setting apart time and attention for Sabbath and prayer shapes our spiritual lives, so does the way in which we prioritize the use of material possessions. Jesus spoke frequently about the relationship between one's possessions and the commitments of the heart. The two are closely connected, which is why Christians speak of setting aside a predetermined amount that belongs to God alone: the tithe. This biblical standard of 10 percent of one's income reflects that our giving to the work of God is proportionate; as we have prospered, so we give. It also recognizes that returning this portion to God is a small reflection of the vast blessing God has given to us first.

To set aside a portion of one's material possessions for God is to prioritize, to order one's commitments, to say with this measure of power called money: this matters to me! If this matters in this way, if I support the mission of my church, give selflessly when I could have kept it all, respond to the need of others rather than indulging in one more luxury for myself, I begin to be ruled by kingdom values and not my own needs. My giving is a sign of my surrender to the higher calling of God in my life.

But what if you haven't really begun your journey toward a mature stewardship? In that case there is no day like today to begin. Begin, for example, by determining what 1 percent of your salary is and giving that to your community of worship. Year by year move that percentage upward until you achieve the joy of tithing. You will never know what freedom this represents until you arrive there. The surprise that awaits you will be the way the joy of giving multiplies in a generous heart. At the end of your life you will discover a great satisfaction in knowing you have left an inheritance, perhaps through your will or estate in addition to the tithes and offerings you've given through your life, to the work of the Lord. Your Christian stewardship can literally outlive you.

In a broader sense, Christians are stewards of all that God has given to our care. This includes the lives of those who depend on us, the creation and environment that is our home, and other species who are vulnerable to our encroachment on their natural homes. Through faith we become humble and grateful managers of this gift of creation, treating it with the care we would desire for ourselves, taking no action that might harm the generations that will follow us.

Because happiness does not subsist in possessions and because concern for the well-being of a neighbor is a part of our faith, we Christians strive to live simply, not consuming more than we need, and tending the garden of the earth in such a way that resources are available to all of God's children.

Many Gifts, One Spirit

If there is one way that we simultaneously identify our unique purpose as a Christian and edify the body of the Church, it is in identifying our God-apportioned gifts and then using them. If the community of Christian believers is like a body, with each member serving in a particular capacity, then no part of the body is dispensable. We all have unique gifts of service to offer, and this diversity of gifts creates the faithful congregation. No person of faith possesses all of the gifts; they are apportioned individually by the Spirit for the upbuilding of the whole church.

If I am searching for my place in God's purpose, one of the starting places in my quest will be to find what gift of service God has given me for this time of life. Not everyone is meant to be a preacher or healer or teacher. But you *have* been given some gift or gifts for building up the body of Christ. And what's more, those gifts may change over the course of your life. God may be giving you a whole new path of service and serenity that just a few years ago you might not have imagined.

Lifelong Learning and Growing

If one thing characterizes the growing Christian life, it is the continuing thirst for spiritual knowledge and deepening of the spirit. Active Christians always seek greater light and understanding. This understanding most often comes through their mutual study of the scriptures with other Christians; a program of ongoing devotional reading; and new exploration of challenging ethical, moral, and social issues of the day as seen through the eyes of faith.

All this translates into Christians who make it a priority to participate in an adult church school class, book study, a midweek Bible study, individual reading, continuing education classes through a nearby seminary, or an occasional series dealing with spiritual growth and discipleship. Your progress will not automatically happen unless you partner with God's Spirit in making it so. This requires spiritual work and commitment.

A Different Kind of Purpose

Faithful communities of Christ and individual Christians place themselves at the disposal of God, striving to discern and then surrender to the purposes of God as they act in the world. Faithfulness to the mission of God requires a multifaceted outward movement toward the neighbor. For this reason the individual Christian can never live in isolation from the whole body of the church, and the church cannot live in isolation from the world.

The early church clearly understood this mission to include a commission from the risen Christ: to go to all the world, proclaiming the good news, teaching the wisdom of Jesus, and baptizing those who respond in faith. In the church we refer to this as *evangelism*, or carrying the evangel. In the Greek text the *evangelion* is simply the announcement or proclamation of good news. We have great, glad news to share about what God is doing with and for us, and it is to be shared with all who would receive it. Some Christians may have been given a special gift of bringing the evangel, but all Christians are called to bring this witness through their words and actions. The day you were baptized, you became an evangelist.

You may be thinking, *Oh, no, I'm not becoming one of those.* Don't worry, no one expects you to. You can put away the characterizations of evangelism found in the television evangelists or your friendly neighborhood religious front porch solicitor or the fellow wearing the sandwich board announcing the end.

Carrying the evangel in our culture requires the honest and authentic sharing of your faith in real life relationships. First and foremost it means living a life based on the Gospel, being the

Christian you were called to be, living out the meaning of your baptism. That example of loving faithfulness will go far to reach even those who are hardened to a simple conversation about faith. Before a conversation ever takes place they will be watching you, assessing your integrity. They will first observe the fruit of the Spirit and later discern a bit about the source of the fruit itself. This evangelism requires a higher than average commitment on the part of the Christian to a life of fairness, honesty, selflessness, compassionate regard for others, and practicing the spiritual disciplines.

Practicing Christians will not shy away from declining an invitation to a Sunday morning activity by simply saying that "our family worships on Sunday morning." When your child's soccer team schedules its practices on Sunday morning, you will decline, request an alternate time, and perhaps rethink participation on the team. Why? Because you are a practicing Christian family.

We do not hesitate to say to our children, "We do this because it is the Christian way."

When the family across the street loses a loved one, we are the first ones there to offer consolation. If we have children, we take them along and explain why we are doing this. We engage in the social ministry of the church as a family not only to model and teach our children how to do so, but also because we are a part of the Christian household and this is our way. We teach our children how to give to the church by beginning instruction on tithing when they are young. Everyone receives an offering envelope. We discuss the values presented through media or advertising and measure them by our Christian convictions. When politicians or governments make decisions, we evaluate them by the gospel. Our identity is decidedly Christian.

When a friend or coworker or extended family member or acquaintance asks about our faith, we don't avoid the discussion; we give a simple account of what we believe and why. When a searching soul turns to us for guidance, we do not hesitate to invite them to our community of faith for worship or a study group or special series. We do this because we are offering them a spiritual cup of water to quench their inner thirst.

To carry the evangel in our culture, to be evangelists, often means swimming upstream and sometimes taking positions not in sync with the majority of the population. We expect resistance to our ideas and values and do not expect that our convictions will always win the admiration of the crowd. We communicate this to our children and teach them how to hold strong convictions, even when they are unpopular.

To be an evangelist, to carry the unusual good news of Jesus who proclaimed a kingdom that comes to outcasts and sinners, also means that we bring good news to the poor and release to the captives, those living on the edge of life, the ones whose lives have caved in, the people who have been moved to the margins. Because we view these persons as children of God, we demonstrate unusual compassion and care to them. We lead with love and build up with hope.

This outward reach of the evangel extends to neighbors across town and to neighbors across the world. We share the good news locally and globally. Not all of us have been called to serve as missionaries outside of our own city or region or country. But some of us have received that distinctive call to a service beyond our borders. In those cases, the best way we can honor God's mission is by extending remarkable support to make their mission on Christ's behalf possible.

Most of all, in our congregations and families, we want our guests to enter the house, look around at our people, and say, "These are a people who know Jesus, who humbly walk as his disciples, and their lives are different as a result. I want to be a part of this household of faith."

The Compassionate Way

Because God entered into the world's suffering through Christ, we enter into the suffering of the neighbor with the Spirit of Christ. For Christians living by the love of Christ, this means not only extending the compassionate reach to the human need that we see and is close at hand. The test of compassion is how we can enable a response to suffering, poverty, natural disaster, racism, and war out of our sight lines. This requires a more selfless compassion because we do not expect immediate gratification from our actions. Our most effective response to the large humanitarian challenges of our time often requires a great degree of trust in organized ministries that are particularly equipped to address situations of great magnitude.

A visionary compassion, however, not only addresses the results of suffering; it also goes upstream to address the causes that create suffering in the first place. Compassion supports and ministers to families who become sick due to polluted water sources, but a visionary compassion addresses just why and how the water is polluted in the first place. Compassion provides shelter for the homeless, but a visionary compassion asks why the homelessness exists in the first place and how fair and adequate housing might be pursued. Compassion visits the prisoner, but a visionary compassion asks how racism continues to shape employment practices, crime, and incarceration. Compassion provides support for the poor woman who has developed breast cancer, but a visionary compassion works toward access to preventive medical care for all before it is too late. Compassion gives emergency food when needed, but a visionary compassion finds ways to provide adequate job training to insure future security and income. The impulse toward compassion is a godly one. The determination to go upstream to address the sources of suffering is both godly and wise.

Prophets, Not Soothsayers

When you hear the word *prophet* what do you think of immediately? For many the word conjures up thoughts of for-tunetellers and clairvoyant seers of the future. When it comes to the classic definition of the prophet in the biblical story, you can put away your crystal balls and tarot cards.

The prophet, in the biblical story, is the one who stands outside the dominant culture, listens to God's word, and then critiques the culture. This critique includes suggestions as to the consequences: If you continue on this course, the inevitable will happen to you. Or perhaps already has. But if you turn away from your present course and honor God, instead, disaster will be averted.

Jesus stood in the prophetic tradition in many respects. He pronounced the judgment of God upon the injustice of the world system in general and on the dominant religious system in particular. These were not of God and would perish, but the reign and kingdom of God would reign forever and ever.

The biblical prophets were keenly aware of injustice and spoke against it on behalf of those least able to speak for themselves. Injustice is always a sign of sin, the tearing of the social fabric, the abuse of some at the hands of others who hold greater power. Because God lifts up the needy, outcast, poor, widow, orphan, and the stranger, the prophet decries all who would abuse them. Because God demands a relationship of fidelity with people of the covenant, their lives become fractured and broken when they abandon the way for idols that masquerade as God.

Today the way of the prophet is exceedingly complex. Networks of power, influence, and oppression span governments, globalized enterprise, wealth, power, and privilege. Rapid change, vast electronic communications systems, and broad scientific research in areas that potentially determine life or death make the moral climb a steep and baffling one.

The church, as an aggregate of the body of Christ and carrier of a moral vision, must speak with prophetic authority, without presuming infallibility, whenever and wherever injustice is found. The unique Christian voice must be brought to bear in the global marketplace of ideas, articulating values and principles that inform ethical decision making. At the least the church must raise the ethical questions the culture may choose to ignore. These may include an extremely broad range of issues, everything from stem cell research to issues of war and peace, sexuality to racism, and family life to environmental degradation.

Of the greatest importance is the passion and clarity the body of Christ brings to casting a vision of God's realm, which stands in contrast to the way of life we are more naturally inclined to create. As we continue to share a vision of God's realm, God's intent for the world, we measure everything else by it. That sometimes leads to correcting the distorted versions of reality by which we presently live. This is our primary prophetic calling.

Everyone Has a Vocation

The root of the word *vocation* comes from the Latin *vocare,* "to call." Christians are all called and have a calling. But what form does this take?

On the most basic level we each have a primary call to faith. We are called to respond to the love and grace of God, revealed in the life of Christ, the power of which transforms us. That is the first calling. In general terms our calling translates into taking the Christian way into all facets of life: family, friendships, work, community, and church. We are called to be Christians everywhere.

One's particular calling is more difficult to discern. Because your job does not necessarily equal your calling, though it may, your real calling may actually be avocational, something other than what you do to make a living. Many artists work nondescript jobs to make their bread and butter in order to pursue their art, which is their real vocation. I may work nine to five to pay the bills, but my real vocation is at the community food pantry. Though my income-producing job may not reflect my real calling, I do want its aims, purposes, and practices to reflect the moral and ethical standards of my faith. If these two ever come into conflict, if my security needs are not in sync with my religious values, I may at some point have to make a hard decision.

A particular calling, on the other hand, is that work, way of life, or path of service for which you believe you were born. This may mean a particular call to direct Christian service, such as congregational ministry, overseas mission work, campus ministry, prison chaplaincy, theological education, community-based Christian benevolent programs, Christian education specialties, ecumenical councils, or a church-based organization for advocacy. This may also mean a particular call to work with the elderly, care for children, teach college students, provide legal representation for those who cannot afford it, practice medicine in an underserved area, help teach English as a second language, teach a Sunday school class, or lead the children's choir. God has a special vocation for you, one that may not be typical or have high visibility.

During the course of life your vocation may and will change. God uses us in different ways as we move through the journey of life. That means your calling may shift and change directions. You may be doing something entirely different ten years from now. And what you are doing now may in fact be tempering you, preparing you for your next calling.

With the longevity of life increasing and people enjoying longer retirements, many find that the later chapters of life are full of new vocational opportunities. Free from the demands of work, retirees may more freely explore and respond to new callings of joyful service. Early retirement and later retirement holds a whole new kingdom potential for God, a yet-to-be tapped source of Christian commitment power.

How do I know? That's the hard question, of course. Finding this calling requires patient discernment, a humble seeking after the will of God. Trusted mentors often see your calling before you do, and you need to seek their council. Experimenting with various forms of ministry to which you are drawn helps as you "try on" different roles, ministry, and service. And much of the time your vocation finds you. As we wait with open eyes and hearts, our future calling often presents itself to us, and we are not infrequently surprised!

For Further Reflection

Exodus 20:8–11	Keeping the sabbath
Matthew 6:5–13	Living in prayer
Luke 21:1–4	Practicing stewardship

1 Corinthians 12:4–31   Claiming the gifts
Matthew 28:16–20   Sharing the good news
Matthew 25:31–45   Extending compassion
Micah 6:6–8   Doing justice

8

Christian Hope and the Future

People live by hope. But just take a minute to reflect on the kinds of hope different people might have.

Different Kinds of Hope

The woman is ninety-eight years old and is now living in a nursing home. She is alert, faithful, and curious as she thinks about her future. The "in the world" part of her life is now behind her. For what does she hope?

The teenage guy is working summers to save enough money to travel to New Mexico, buy the necessary gear, and arrange lessons for rock climbing. It's a dream of his. Someday soon he wants to be on that rock face. What kind of hope does he have?

The parents watch as their grown child is flushing life down the toilet of drugs. Everything is falling apart: work, relationships, and happiness. But somewhere in the midst of it all they find some reason for encouragement. They have hope that this whole mess will turn around.

The serviceman is stationed far from home. He's been watching his brothers in arms fall one by one. Only one month remains in his tour. A wife and baby await him back home. He hopes that all goes well and that he'll be with them by Christmas.

Hope. We all need it. People die without it. And it's the most elusive thing imaginable. What is it, and where do you find it?

Christian Hope's Distinction

Though frequently confused with psychological conditions, attitudes, or moods, Christian hope is something distinctive. Christian hope is not the same thing as positive thinking and its resulting attitude toward life. Positive thinking can be important, but it is not Christian hope. Christian hope is not the same thing as optimism. Thinking of the glass as half-full rather than half-empty makes life a lot more enjoyable, but it is not Christian hope. Christian hope is not the same as having a can-do attitude. That personality characteristic contributes to success in many areas, but it is not Christian hope. Christian hope is not the same as wishfulness. I may wish for something to be the way I want it to be, but that is not Christian hope. Christian hope is not the same as believing in fate. The notion of fate is a pagan, not a Christian conviction. It is easy to simply resign oneself to a pre-scripted course of events, but that is not Christian hope. Christian hope is not the same as believing time takes care of everything. In and of itself, time does nothing. What happens *within* time is what matters. It is not the same as Christian hope.

Christian Hope as Trust in the Saving God

Christian hope is solidly lodged in trust of what God will be and do. Christian hope is oriented toward the future, but not just any future. Christian hope is the sure and certain trust that the future belongs to God and that, therefore, as we travel into the future we travel into God. And those convictions about God and the future create hopeful souls; we are neither terrified nor apathetic.

The language of the Bible contains many uses and variants of the word *salvation*. In fact, a whole subset of theology called *soteriology* just thinks about that. It is based on the Greek word, *soter*, meaning "savior." How does God save people?

Hebrew scripture mostly speaks of salvation in regard to deliverance; God saves me from suffering, calamity, and death.

That's why, for instance, when Jesus rides into Jerusalem on Palm Sunday expectant Jews chant, "Hosanna to the son of David." Hosanna means "he saves." They are looking for deliverance from their cruel Roman occupation and a restoration of the throne of David.

The prayer language of the Psalms includes many references to salvation, the remembrance of or hope for God's deliverance. Because God has proved faithful in the past, we trust God in the future. We are hopeful because God saves us. In the Christian message hope also includes God's deliverance in history. But there is more.

When Christians refer to Christ as *soter,* or savior, they express an understanding that we are saved from many things in many ways. For instance, if the problem is ignorance of God, then Christ saves us from that ignorance with saving knowledge. If the problem is sin and brokenness, then Christ saves through reconciliation and healing. And if the final threat is death itself, Christ saves us as the one who was the first fruits of they who slept. The power of death has not overcome because of new life and resurrection; therefore, we have hope in the God that saves us ultimately.

Christian Hope as Continuing Hope

If you look carefully at the writings of the New Testament, the concept of salvation is not limited to a one-time event. Salvation is not limited to a onetime alteration of the condition of the soul. Rather, it is something God continues to do. God is always in the act of saving. We, on the other hand, awaken to or grow into the realization that the God who created me continues to save the whole created world, including me. It's a process.

Christians also have a robust hope based on God's future beyond death. Because our present existence is not the end of the story but rather one chapter of it, we are filled with hope. Christians in different times and places have talked about, explained, and described this ultimate future with God in many ways.

The gospel of John and also some of the letters of Paul reflect an implied understanding that upon one's personal death the faithful will immediately be in the presence of God. Death is like passing through a thin membrane into the unseen reality of God. Alongside this understanding of personal immortality is an equally strong conviction of a general resurrection of all people at the end of history.

How does one reconcile these two understandings? On the one hand Jesus says to one of the thieves on a cross beside him that *today* the thief will join him in paradise. On the other hand the Bible speaks about the coming of the Son of Man *at the end* when all stand before the judgment throne. Which one is correct?

Of course, you can't solve a conundrum like this. But you may have to choose. You may decide that one passes to the presence of God at death, and that in a way the end of your personal world is what all of the language about the end of the world or the end of history is really about—the end of your personal world. If you decide there is a general resurrection at the end of world history, then you might remind yourself that the passing of time is nothing for those sleeping in death A thousand years are but a second in God's time; the end is already here.

In either case, you must place yourself into the hands of the God of the future, trusting in death as you have in life.

Christian Hope as Apocalyptic Hope

Many Jews and Christians of the first century anticipated a cataclysmic end to the world in which God would triumph, evil would be overcome, and the faithful delivered. The writings of this time and style are called apocalyptic writings. The most conspicuous example of the genre is the last book of the New Testament called the Revelation of John. This unique kind of biblical literature stands in contrast to other ways of viewing God working in history.

John was an ecstatic seer, one who wrote of his visions and revelations and lived on the old Roman penal colony island of Patmos. There he wrote a letter directed to the Christian congregations located in present-day Greece and Turkey. In his vision he described the heavy oppression of persecuted Christians and how, in the end, God would triumph and evil would be overcome. These Christians lived by nothing but hope.

Through the centuries, Christians have read such visions of the future in Revelation and also in the letters of the apostle Paul and found hope, encouragement, and courage to trust in God. Though the early expectation of Christians was that the end would come soon, even in their lifetimes, they still held on to the conviction that in the end God would fulfill the good creation, even if it were postponed to an indefinite future. Someday the waters of the river of life would run through a new and transformed reality in which God would shine as the only light of the people.

Leaving behind the Problems of Dispensationalism

One of the problems present day Christians have with considering God's future is that one form of interpreting these apocalyptic texts has become exceedingly popular. In the nineteenth century some people attempted to impose their own "grids" of interpretation on them. One of these grids was called *dispensationalism*, a recent development in the history of Christianity. This philosophy of interpreting the texts depended on carving up history into dispensations, or units, and then attributing different parts of scripture to this arbitrary time line. One could, according to this system, chart out the course of historical events and predict when certain things would happen. The system included a portrait of the end of the world and how believing Christians are involved in it. Dispensationalism is the main philosophy and theology of the wildly popularized and lucrative *Left Behind* series.

Left Behind theology, which is really nineteenth-century dispensationalism warmed over, presents several problems. First, history is not really carved up this way. That is the fiction of this movement. This system attempts to paint the unpredictable God into a box, determining all outcomes as though God cannot change course along the way. Second, this model of faith is pre-occupied with figuring out a code and then watching your calendar. That is the old science carving up reality into measurable bits again. It reduces faith to believing in a system rather than radically trusting God. Third, and most importantly, this appeals not to Christian hope but to human fears. Those captured by this system flee punishment but miss the saving grace.

One of the frequent byproducts of this version of apocalyptic theology is the discounting of any work towards justice and peace. This way of thinking diminishes our responsibility to affirm, work for, and protect the world and all its inhabitants: If a conflagration is what is necessary to unleash the final apocalypse, then let us hasten the conflict. If Armageddon is inevitable in the Middle East, it is not important if our actions generate conflict or insta-bility—we welcome the day. If this world is simply crashing toward a massive conflagration then we don't really have to be stewards and caretakers of our environment; we may recklessly spoil it with no thought of our impact on future generations. Why not, if the end is so near and will come in this way? Besides, we will be snatched away from the catastrophe anyway, spared the suffering and the flames. In case of the rapture, this car will be unmanned—careening, we suppose into the path of others who are...left behind.

What you need to know is that this is only one way of reading the text, and a suspect one at that. And it is also only one narrow way of viewing the way God is or acts in the world. It is a recent development in Christianity. And what is wildly popular at the moment is neither superior nor enduring.

If you have found yourself holding back from following the Christian way because you find this *Left Behind* theology highly objectionable, be reassured: You don't have to believe it to be a Christian. The really good news is that Christians can leave behind the *Left Behind* theology and still have a lively trust and hope in God. The future belongs to God and will materialize in ways out of human control. Not even the angels know the future, says Jesus. Why should you?

Christian Hope as Certain Victory

This is God's universe. We belong to God. Our future is wrapped up in the future of God. In Christ we are convinced of a powerful victory over death and, indeed, our salvation is always at hand. Be of good cheer. Take hope.

The center of the Christian proclamation is nowhere found with more clarity than in the apostle Paul's first letter to the Corinthian church. In the fifteenth chapter of this correspondence lies the golden nugget of the faith. It is a core message Paul himself received and was in turn passing on to the faithful. The outlines of the message are clear and simple: Christ died for our sins, was buried, raised on the third day, and then appeared to Peter, the twelve, and an expanded group of followers.

In the speaking of these words the power of God is unleashed to overcome the power of sin and death. In remembering how God spoke and acted, we know God speaking and acting now. In the fellowship of the witnesses, we experience the Risen One mysteriously present among us.

So the first word spoken about hope, the future, and the resurrection has to do with the exaltation of Christ. Because Christ is raised, we have hope in the power of God.

The second word, by extension, is one about our own destiny in Christ. Paul weaves a cosmic tapestry, a portrait of God's redeeming action in the future. In the end, when time as we know it comes to a close, the dead will be raised imperishable. In the twinkling of an eye, he says, we shall be changed, transformed. In the same way that the form of an acorn must give way to becoming its tree, so our physical, mortal lives must pass away in order that a totally different reality may come. It will be nothing like the form of what we experience now, so we only have metaphors and poetry to express the inexpressible.

How do you express an alternate reality with God, a different dimension, a future way of being that is unknown? Only by appealing to what you do know. It is your only frame of reference. You dare to speak even as you know that words are entirely inadequate. And the writers of scripture faced one and the same challenge: They had to use the only thoughts, images, and language they had at their disposal to speak of the great mystery. It is not enough, of course, but it is all we have as long as we peer through this darkened, cloudy glass.

After struggling to help this small group of Christians embrace the resurrection power, at the end of his words and ideas, Paul the proclaimer bursts into doxology, a song of praise and victory that circulated among the earliest Christian communities:

> Death has been swallowed up in victory.
> Where, O death, is your victory?
> Where, O death, is your sting? (1 Cor. 15:54–55)

With such faith and hope, with such trust in a God who acted and acts, we commit our future to the God of the future, the Lord of heaven and earth. The One who created still creates. The One who loved the world into being continues to redeem it until all is in all. The One who loves us draws us into a new life—now and forever.

For Further Reflection

Luke 23:39–43	Today you will be with me in paradise
1 Corinthians 15:3–11, 35–55	We shall be changed
Hebrews 12:1–2	The cloud of witnesses
Revelation 21:1–4	The new Jerusalem

Postscript

Like most kids growing up in a religious community, I went along for the ride. It's not that I had any special aversion to religious life, church, and all that went along with it. My family was a practicing Christian family, and that's what we did. It was normal.

My earliest memories of participating in a religious community include locating my parents' adult class that always had donuts. Boy, were they good. But I also remember my own Sunday school classes, vacation Bible school, and singing in the choir. They are vague, foggy memories; but they shaped me in unusual ways that make more sense to me now.

The first time that I "got" the religious thing was sitting in a worship service, looking up at the ceiling while the congregation was singing, and trying to count all the light bulbs. I happened to have a parent sitting on each side of me, trapped as I was in the pew, walls of big shoulders to left and right with no escape and no brother within reach to torment. And I remember just looking to left and right, to mother and father, and observing them at worship. I saw my mother's expression of joy, my father cocking his head to the left when he heard an intriguing idea in the sermon. What I saw was something I hadn't noticed before: the two most important people in my life caught up in wonder and awe. And I said to myself, *I am in the presence of something really big.*

Because my job up to age twelve was being a kid, I focused on doing it well. Like others I went to school, played in the evening, played baseball, threw snowballs, avoided homework, and watched my favorite television shows. The spiritual thing was like a background track to a movie: present and supporting everything else. And then one Sunday morning when I was around twelve, our family was in worship. At the conclusion of the sermon, which I couldn't recount for you if my life depended on it, the preacher issued a call to discipleship: "If you will accept this Jesus as Lord and commit yourself to the way of God, come now and profess that publicly, and do not delay." In my young mind I heard myself saying, *Well, yes. Now or never.* To my unsuspecting parents' surprise, I stood up, walked down the aisle, and gave my life to this mysterious Jesus.

It's a blur, of course, but I do remember how it moved my parents and how all the old ladies fawned all over me and the normally slaphappy men were wiping little tears out of the corner of their eyes. I thought to myself, *I'm in the presence of something really big.*

I was baptized in a worship service the next Sunday. What surprised me was that I was asked to go into this little changing room, strip naked, and slip into this white baptismal gown with weights sewn into the bottom hem. I thought that weights and swimming were not a good idea together, but I soon realized they were meant to keep the gown from billowing up under the water.

The water was cold, really cold, and I was awakened in more ways than one. I remember wading out into that pool and just before plunging to my death in Christ hearing the preacher say, "I baptize you in the name of the Father, Son, and Holy Spirit." There was a big splash and, unlike my swimming at the community pool, it was followed with holy communion. I remember the hands that served me communion held a tray just about at eye level.

During my adolescence I had stops and starts with my spiritual life. Along with sports, music, and girls the background track of faith kept on playing. Standouts had to do with special youth opportunities like musicals and drama and camps. These special times apart spoke to my young heart. I was surrounded by admired mentors who served as role models for me. These were caring people living out the faith. Through them I could put two and two together.

By the time college rolled around I was testing the spiritual waters in almost every way. My college classes were stimulating and pushed on the edges I was pushing on too. Teachers and ministers and chaplains during that time helped me develop an intellectually challenging faith. I started reading and discussing ideas that had seemed taboo only a short time before. No subject was out of consideration.

In my college years I tended to run from the campus organizations that offered pat little answers to faith; I was heading the other direction. I was challenging all the presuppositions. I surrounded myself with secular people who found me an oddity, a Christian who liked them and would even talk to them about things they didn't believe. One of the greatest signs came when an atheist friend said of my religious aspirations, "If anyone else had told me this stuff, I would have told them they were full of bull hockey." It was the clearest message from God I had received to date.

After spending a summer serving as a youth director in a small church and a year of teaching in a public school, the background track of faith moved once and for all to the foreground. My minister mentor took me to lunch and popped the question about ministry. I was speechless. Not that I hadn't asked myself about that before, or timidly shared the thought with parents in my early life, but the thought that someone else was seeing in me what I wondered about myself was overwhelming.

I left that lunch with barbecue sauce on my chin and a knot in my throat. It wouldn't be long until I enrolled in seminary. I had no idea where that journey would take me.

Seminary was full of incredible moments, both academic and spiritual. I was surprised by the richness of community life in a place forming people for ministry. On the same day I could hear a lecture about form criticism in Biblical studies, listen to provocative preaching in seminary chapel, and eat lunch with classmates as we discussed ministry in the church. Sometimes I floated in a kind of mental and emotional fog, piecing together my reconstructed faith.

Finally the time came when seminary concluded. And then came my ordination, the church setting me aside for a particular ministry in the body. I remember kneeling in the chancel of the sanctuary and feeling the weight of hands being placed upon my head. I remember the weight of the mantle of ministry being placed upon my life. And I said to myself, *I'm in the presence of something really big.*

Since that time, I've served in both a county seat town and in metropolitan areas. People are people and mess up their lives. Examples of faithful living abound. The church alternately inspires and disappoints. I've changed. My thinking has changed. I've traveled to places where Christians are doing amazing things in mission and witness. In all this I have been amazed that God just keeps clicking right along in a billion ways. One of the great discoveries of ministry and faith has been that my main calling is to find where God is at work and then just join in. I don't create it; I agree to enter the dance. That's a hard lesson to learn. But it's a good one.

One of my greatest hopes is that, in time, I will become like some of my most treasured, respected, and beloved mentors, both lay and clergy. I am certain I will be very, very old if I ever attain this. But then again, God does the attaining.

In a sense my whole life has been an attempt to fulfill the meaning of my baptism. My whole ministry has been an attempt to fulfill the meaning of my ordination. And I have never made steady, uninterrupted progress on either score. I've been faithful to those callings and sometimes not. The fire of the commitment has burned unevenly over time. But even so, God's tender mercy is such that I have been allowed, by degrees, to surrender more and more to God's astounding grace.

My greatest hope for you is that in the course of your life you will find yourself astounded before the majesty and mystery of God such that you will exclaim with a humble and thankful heart, "I'm in the presence of something really big."